Dr. Payal Chadha

Financial Performance of Companies listed on the Kuwait Stock Exchange

An Exploration using
Altman's Z-Score Model

Anchor Academic
Publishing

Chadha, Payal: Financial Performance of Companies listed on the Kuwait Stock Exchange. An Exploration using Altman's Z-Score Model, Hamburg, Anchor Academic Publishing 2016

Buch-ISBN: 978-3-96067-043-8
PDF-eBook-ISBN: 978-3-96067-543-3
Druck/Herstellung: Anchor Academic Publishing, Hamburg, 2016

Bibliografische Information der Deutschen Nationalbibliothek:
Die Deutsche Nationalbibliothek verzeichnet diese Publikation in der Deutschen Nationalbibliografie; detaillierte bibliografische Daten sind im Internet über http://dnb.d-nb.de abrufbar.

Bibliographical Information of the German National Library:
The German National Library lists this publication in the German National Bibliography. Detailed bibliographic data can be found at: http://dnb.d-nb.de

© Anchor Academic Publishing, Imprint der Diplomica Verlag GmbH
Hermannstal 119k, 22119 Hamburg
http://www.diplomica-verlag.de, Hamburg 2016
Printed in Germany

Abstract

A quantitative method was used to explore the financial performance of the listed firms on the Kuwait Stock Exchange. The number of firms explored was 196 out of a possible 206 (two firms are subsidiaries of one of the firm, and others are insurance firms excluded from this study). The listed firms were observed from 2009-2014 to understand their status in the market, and the direction they are headed towards. The financial data were gathered from the published annual reports of the respective firms and the financial statements from the Kuwait Stock Exchange website. The results, using the Altman Z-score model for the period 2009-2014, show that approximately 39.46% of the firms on average were safe; approximately 25.94% of the firms on average were distressed; approximately 15.90% of the firms on average were in a grey area; and approximately 18.71% firms on average had no available data. The bankruptcy rate could not be justified using the Zmijewski score model due to the inconclusive results and the absence of bankruptcy laws in the State of Kuwait. The financially secure sectors, which are good for investment, are petroleum and consumer goods (i.e., food, slaughterhouses, banks, and parallel markets). The worst performers that continue to operate despite the losses are real estate, telecommunications, and investment firms. This study provides insight into the financial distress level in Kuwait. The level of distress shows that major changes are necessary within firms and operations are not running smooth. Bankruptcy laws are required for firms operating in distress. This exploration is a stepping-stone for potential investors by showing the most profitable sectors for investment and for future researchers to predict accurate bankruptcy rates in the State of Kuwait.

Key words: bankruptcy, distress, firm, Altman Z-score, Zmijewski score, model, stock market, Kuwait

1

Acknowledgements

The lettering of this academic paper has been one of the most momentous intellectual challenges This is the hardest thing I have ever faced. Without the support, persistence and direction of the following populace, this learning could not have been finished. It is to them I owe my deepest gratitude.

- Dr. Igor Gvozdanovic, who undertook to act as my mentor, despite his other academic and qualified commitments. His intelligence, knowledge and commitment to the highest standards inspired and motivated me.
- I am grateful for the support and advice from the faculty of Swiss Management Center University.
- My colleague at work, Dipika Mahuvarker, for always boosting my confidence.
- To my invaluable network of supportive, sympathetic, liberal and affectionate friends, without whom I could not have survived the process: Jae Remy, Joseph Gonsalves, Trevor D'souza, Saurabh S, Saqib Umer, Tariq Iqbal, and others for encouraging my efforts.
- My parents Nisha and Mumtaz, and two younger brothers, Divyanshu and Sershar, who have always supported, encouraged and believed in me, in all my endeavors.
- Last, God, who has always answered my prayers and never let me down whenever I took up a decision to pursue something.

Table of Contents

List of Figures

List of Tables

List of Abbreviations

ATS	Alternative Trading System
CA	Current Assets
CL	Current Liabilities
EBIT	Earnings before Interest and Taxes
GCC	Gulf Cooperation Council
ICB	International Classification Benchmark
KSE	Kuwait Stock Exchange
NI	Net Income
RE	Retained Earnings
SMC	Swiss Management Centre
TA	Total Assets
TE	Total Equity
TL	Total Liabilities

Dedication

This paper is devoted to my mother who believed in my hard work and determination. As Patrick Driessen quotes, to do everything with love, passion and dedication. This motto inherited from my mom helped me accomplish this academic success.

This paper is dedicated to my family, friends, and colleagues.

Chapter 1: Overview

This research studied the financial performance of the listed companies on the Kuwait Stock Exchange. This study explored whether the Kuwait market is good for investment by foreign investors to trade in stocks. Because such a study has not been conducted before, this study presents limitations, such as lack of and unavailable data. The study presents opportunities of investment available in various sectors for potential foreign investors and further develops an understanding of the future of the Kuwait Stock Market. This study used quantitative research methodology to investigate the financial performance of the Kuwait market via Altman's Z-score model and Zmijewski's bankruptcy model. Annual reports of the listed companies and financial statements from the Kuwait Stock Exchange website were used for examination.

Problem Statement

The main problem is that financial markets have been recurrently crashing e.g., stock market collapse in China. Such phenomenon affects the markets worldwide. For investors, it is difficult to predict such phenomena. However, they can invest sensibly by using the bankruptcy prediction models for judging the firm's financial condition.

The Kuwait financial market was limited due to its lack of maturity and depth, lack of imposed restrictions, and overseas investment in the stock market portfolios did not have the sufficient attention until the early nineties. These foreign investments are viewed as "hot money", and the government preferred direct investments (Kuwait Stock Exchange, n.d.).

Kuwait has opened its market for attracting foreign assets with the associated repayment to the economy of Kuwait by contributing to the national projects and transferring the latest technological developments (Kuwait Stock Exchange, n.d.). The core intention of the foreign investors is to maximize proceeds while guaranteeing their rights in the legislative framework.

Thus, the restrictions were eradicated on work permits and ownerships, and the clashes in the related laws and regulations (Kuwait Stock Exchange, n.d.). In 1999, the Amiree Decree Law No. 10 was issued regarding the directive of the direct investment of foreign assets in Kuwait. This investment committee studies the investment needs, sponsors the vacant venture occasions in the country, presents incentives to persuade overseas investors, smoothens the progress of licensing events, and gets rid of the obstacles which the foreign investors might face (Kuwait Securities House K.S.C.C., n.d.).

In 2000, the Amiree decree No. 20 was issued for the approval of foreign investors to possess shares in the shareholding companies of Kuwait that exist or may be established (Al – Yaqout, 2013). According to the ministerial decree No. 205, the inner bylaws of the non-direct speculation in securities law was issued, which regulates foreign investor's investment in stocks (Kuwait Securities House K.S.C.C., n.d.).

In 2008, income tax on the earnings of foreign companies was reduced from 55% to 15%, as per law No. 2 and the freedom from taxes on profits from trading on the Kuwait stock market, made straight or through portfolios or investment funds, attracted foreign investment significantly increasing the trading volume in the market (Al-Yaqout, 2013). However, more awareness is needed to attract investors from around the world. This study will help investors analyze the sectors that are performing well, and help the listed firms know of their company status, and take necessary actions to improve their financial image in the eyes of investors.

Purpose of Research

This quantitative study focuses on the financial performance of the companies listed on the Stock Exchange of Kuwait. The purpose is to find out how likely are Kuwait firms to file for bankruptcy and to provide additional and better understanding of Kuwait corporate performance since financial ratios alone are not enough to analyze whether the firms in Kuwait stock market are profitable for foreign investment. The analysis, using the Altman Z-score model and Zmijewski model, helps in predicting which will be the profitable firms and the endangered firms, which is a useful indicator for successful firm acquisition by possibly profitable firms interested in expanding their business. Both tools predict the performance level and bankruptcy level. The intent of this study was to assess the sectors in Kuwait that are suitable for investment with least involved risk. The results will assist future investors in making profitable investment decisions and generating fruitful gains.

Significance of the Study

The significance of the study is to expand the existing research that has been conducted on various financial markets. This exploration creates the initial knowledge and understanding of the future of the Kuwait stock market. Ijaz, Hunjra, Hameed, Maqbool, and Azam (2013) stated that the failure of business causes large financial and non-financial losses. Therefore, an appropriate forecast of the financial health of a business is essential for stakeholders of the business, including clientele (Ijaz, et al., 2013). The study analyzed the performance of the companies listed on Kuwait Stock Exchange using the Altman's Z-score model and Zmijewski score model for any bankruptcy prevalent in the upcoming future. This analysis helps CEOs understand whether investing in Kuwait Stocks is profitable as Kuwaiti Dinar (KWD) is relatively strong when compared to the currencies of other Gulf countries. This is a good sign for generating higher profits in the stock market. So far, no such study has been conducted on the Kuwait stock market. This study will help foreign investors in understanding this market for making future investments.

Over the years, the initial models of Altman and Zmijewski have been altered based on the firm i.e., manufacturing or non-manufacturing. This study is a stepping-stone for further analysis by future researchers to enhance the Altman Z-score and Zmijewski score models that are best suited to the Middle East countries and other types of firms.

Thus, the study sheds further light on the usage of models like Altman and Zmijewski score among future investors and companies, in testing their financial condition of companies and their investment for mergers and acquisitions, and in further developing the bankruptcy laws in the country of Kuwait so firms can function better.

Research Design

The quantitative research methodology used numerical data from the financial statements. To ensure the accuracy of the secondary data collected, published company annual reports on their individual websites and financial statements from Kuwait Stock Exchange are used. Hence, no primary data was required as the financials used for analysis are published and available for easy access. Muthukumar and Sekar (2014) stated that the Altman Z - score is a quantitative method based on the balance sheet and income statement data for determining a company's financial health. The Zmijewski score model uses probability versus traditional analysis to determine whether the listed companies will go bankrupt in the coming two years. The research design was causal to determine how far the company's performance was affected post-financial crisis. There are 206 companies listed on the Kuwait stock market out of which 196 were explored. The insurance companies were excluded from the study, and two companies are subsidiaries for one of the petroleum firms.

Research Questions (Hypotheses)

The objectives of this research were:

1. Examine the financial soundness of listed companies using the Z - score model in Kuwait from 2009-2014; and

2. Predict the bankruptcy rate of the listed firms within two years using Zmijewski score.

Keeping the above objectives in mind, the intent of the research was to answer the following questions:

R1. Are the firms listed in Kuwait stock market efficient for foreign investment?

If the firm is operating as per the criterion of Altman Z-score and Zmijewski score models, both models go in hand with each other. However, if the firms are operating well under Altman Z-score model criteria and not under Zmijewski score model or vice versa, then they oppose each other's theory aiming towards distress/bankruptcy.

H_{01}: The models Altman's Z-score and Zmijewski's Score do not contradict each other

H_{11}: The models Altman's Z-score and Zmijewski's Score contradict each other.

R2. Is bankruptcy likely to occur in the future in the listed firms of Kuwait stock market?

The Zmijewski score model criterion states that a positive score shows no bankruptcy while a negative score shows bankruptcy in the coming two years.

H_{02}: Bankruptcy does not occur in two years if Zmijewski's Score is positive.

H_{12}: Bankruptcy can occur in two years if Zmijewski's Score is negative.

Assumptions and Limitations

All data gathered in this research was from the yearly reports of the respective company sites and Kuwait Stock Exchange website. This study applied the assumption that the companies are well established and performing well with positive profits as they are listed in the stock exchange. Data from 2009 onwards has been used for this study. The aim was to explore the Kuwait stock market post-financial crisis of 2008. The five-year period 2009-2014 would provide a better scenario of the financial market when compared to one or two years. The limitations that exist in this research are:

- Many firms have no data available for the years 2009 and 2010. The primary reason being they were not established yet. However, this does not affect the Altman results for the individual firms.

- Many firms do not have annual reports published. These firms have used financial statements available from the Kuwait Stock Exchange website.

- Data reports firms for certain years were available in the language of Arabic and have not been used in this study. This was compensated by the financials available on the Kuwait Stock Exchange website.

- For calculation, Net profit of a firm has been used instead of EBIT since data was not available in the statements.

- Some firms did not have data for retained earnings and hence, the calculation scores were incomplete and could be inconclusive. Hence, there could be a discrepancy in categorizing the firms from distressed to grey zone to secure.

Operational Definitions

Altman's Z-score model is a financial model that uses five ratios from the financial statements for determining the likelihood of a company's bankruptcy in the coming two years (The Free Dictionary, 2009).

Asset is defined as a valuable item (The Free Dictionary, 2011).

Bankruptcy is defined as the inability of the firm to pay its debts. This results in reorganization and continued operation of the firm or liquidation and distribution of the proceeds to clear the outstanding amount (Scott, 2003).

14

Distress is defined as a condition of strain (The Free Dictionary, 2011).

Hot Money is defined as the currency that is moved from one form of investment to another, to take advantage of changing international exchange rates or gain (The Free Dictionary, 2011).

Speculation is defined as trading a financial mechanism involving high risk, in expectation of substantial returns. The motive is to maximize gains from fluctuations in the market (Definition of Speculation, n.d.). Speculators are widespread in the markets where price movements of securities are recurrent and unpredictable. They play very important roles in the markets by absorbing excess risk and providing much-needed liquidity in the market by buying and selling when other investors don't take part (Definition of Speculation, n.d.).

Zmijewski model is similar to Altman's Z-score model, i.e. it uses ratios from the financial statements, as the probability unit to predict whether a firm will go bankrupt in two years (YCHARTS, n.d.).

Summary of Overview

The first chapter covers the framework of this study. This research analyzed the financial condition of the firms listed on the Kuwait Stock Exchange. Due to lack of research on this subject, the investors are unaware whether Kuwait is a strong market for investment. The significance of this quantitative research is to use financial tools like the Altman Z-score model and Zmijewski model to predict the performance and bankruptcy level of these firms. More stability of the firms and lesser bankruptcy probability will show the sectors and firms excellent for stock trading. The hypotheses prove whether the Altman Z-score model and Zmijewski model are on the same path together. If true, H_{01} hypothesis is fulfilled. If H_{02} is true, the hypothesis is fulfilled. These models will answer the research questions whether the Kuwait

15

market is efficient for investment as per the Altman Z-score model and if bankruptcy prevails

soon as per the Zmijewski score model. Annual reports of the companies and financial

statements from the Kuwait Stock Exchange website are used for gathering and calculating the

secondary data.

Chapter 2: Literature Review

Before proceeding further into the theoretical set up of this study, it is necessary to position the history of the Kuwait Stock Market. The study forecasts the bankruptcy probability of companies listed on the stock exchange by using financial ratios and probability units. The financial ratios are calculated by using balance sheet data and income statement for each company while the probability units will further be conducted using Microsoft Excel software. This area will then illustrate the conclusions of several papers on the Altman Z-score model and Zmijewski score model by using the financial ratios, and it will be concluded by expanding the existing literature.

Theoretical Orientation

The Gulf Cooperation Council (GCC) is comprised of six Gulf States, namely Bahrain, Kuwait, Oman, Qatar, Saudi Arabia, and the United Arab Emirates, a political and economic pact, pledged to achieve endlessly closer unification (Sikimic, 2015). The stock markets in the GCC are comparatively small, and the majority of stocks are infrequently traded since the trading volume is low (Hassan, Al-Sultan, & Al-Saleem, 2003).

The banking sector accounts for 49%, followed by telecoms with 11% of the total Kuwait Stock Exchange value (World Bank, n.d.). As of September 2014, the capital adequacy ratio in Kuwait's banking industry was 18.3%, up from 15.6% at the end of 2008, and above the minimum requirement of 12% (World Bank, n.d.). Kuwait's sovereign net foreign assets were valued at 269% of GDP at the end of the 2014 – the highest of any rated sovereign, according to Fitch – and government debt was at just 5.3% of GDP, showing Kuwait's strong fiscal position (Oxford Business Group, 2015).

17

Commercial banks control the financial markets in this constituency (Hassan et al., 2003). In 1952, the investors of Kuwait were introduced to stock trades and National Bank of Kuwait was the primary Kuwaiti shareholding company (Kuwait Securities House K.S.C.C., n.d.). In 1976, exploratory trading led to a twist in stock prices and volume in the over-the-counter market until the market failed (Hassan et al., 2003). This led the government to put restrictions on listing of new companies in the stock exchange, by making a forward trade and margin set of laws (Hassan et al., 2003). In 1978, the Kuwait stock market stabilized and led to the creation of Souk Al-Manakh (a parallel stock exchange) in 1979 as an unregulated market in Kuwait, where Gulf-based companies did not meet the exchange listing requirements (Hassan et al., 2003). In August 1983, the Kuwait Stock Exchange was established under the Amiri declaration (Kuwait Securities House K.S.C.C., n.d.). Towards the end of 2001, the top ten listed firms in Kuwait in terms of market capitalization was about 55.5 % of the market capitalization of every listed firm (Omet, & Mashharawe, n.d.). The firms in Kuwait finance their standard economic activities from the local money and capital markets and the "excess" cash is invested in international portfolios (Omet, & Mashharawe, n.d.). On 28th February 2010, the trading activities and regulations were reassigned to the Capital Markets Authority by the latest law (Al-Yaqout, 2013).

The Arab stock markets have witnessed a latest trading environment, because of globalization, liberalization, and the mixing of the world economy, leading to new practices in the majority of stock exchanges (Sabri, 2008). These practices are: the linkages increase in the midst of the world stock markets, an increase in the share of foreign ownership, increase in cross-border stock trading transactions, the use of ATS for stock trading, and the use of the internet to stock trading, which changed the environment from floor trading to screen-based trading (Sabri, 2008). A lot of stocks in the Kuwait Stock Exchange is traded (Hassan et al., 2003).

Kuwait has the following history regarding stock market trading:

- In 1992, the liberalization policies practiced by Kuwait fascinated the Western fund managers in quest of high rates of return and diversification of the portfolio (Hassan et al., 2003).

- In November 1995, first electronic trading system was implemented (Kuwait Stock Exchange, n.d.).

- In October 1998, forwards were established.

- In August 2003, futures were introduced.

- In November 2003, online trading began.

- In March 2005, options started trading.

- In Late 2009, a partnership contract was signed between NASDAQ OMX and Kuwait Stock Exchange, implementing the "X-stream" trading system Phase 1 in 2012.

- In May 2010, the "SMARTS" supervision system was put into operation.

- Phase 2 of the trading system is under process to introduce new items and services, counting ETFs, Futures and Options in the global form, Market makers for suitable products, fixed income instruments, Sukuks, and New indices.

There are a lot of corporate and government bonds and treasury bills traded in the majority of the Arab stock exchanges, and Islamic and conventional bonds (Sabri, 2008). Today, there are numerous mutual Islamic and conventional closed- and open-end funds traded in Arab stock markets, including equities and bond portfolios, with local and foreign currencies (Sabri, 2008).

Kuwait has a longstanding reputation as a center for Islamic financial services, leading to the rapid expansion of sharia-compliant banks and investment companies in recent times. Islamic banking assets, at just over 20% of the total in 2005, grew to around 45% by the end of 2013, and an IMF report released in December 2014 showed Kuwait's sharia-compliant banking sector is the fifth largest in the world, with more than $68.9bn in assets (World Bank, n.d.). The bond market appears poised for a resurgence, with a variety of private and state-owned firms recently announcing plans to issue Sukuk, or sharia-compliant bonds (Oxford Business Group, 2015).

As per the Kuwait Stock Exchange website (n.d.), the market capitalization of Kuwait Stock Exchange has consistently been one of the biggest of Arab markets, in the company of more than 200 companies working out over KD 28 billion (US$100 billion) market value. With a market capitalization to GDP ratio of approximately 100%, the Kuwait Stock Exchange market is unfathomable than its neighbours (Kuwait Stock Exchange, n.d.).

Sharif and Benmeleh (2015) stated the shares volume crashed to 123 million, 49% of the three-month daily average. The sectors that exist in the Kuwait stock market for primary/secondary trading are banking, investment, insurance, real estate, industrial services, food, and non-Kuwaiti. The firms in Kuwait with growth opportunities have higher debt ratios because they can get the debt finance whenever needed (Omet, & Mashharawe, n.d.). The primary market involves the IPOs which can be bought by Kuwaitis only, when the company goes public. The secondary market involves the purchase of shares from existing investors (Ayms, 2010).

The following changes occurred in the market in Kuwait (Kuwait Stock Exchange, n.d.):

- Closing prices were calculated in a closing auction (Kuwait Stock Exchange, n.d.).

- Bids made use of price/time priority.

- Firms were placed into sectors by the International Classification Benchmark (a product of FTSE International Limited and certified for use by KSE).

- The "Kuwait 15" index was introduced KSX15 for sustaining a variety of inventive products and services.

- New order types were supported by the trading system GTC and GTD

According to a report titled, "Dealing with Bankruptcy in the GCC", issued by Kuwait Financial Centre (2013), bankruptcy laws in Kuwait are still pending. This report stated that as of March 2009, after the financial crisis, the Financial Stability Law (FSL) was introduced. However, issues regarding bankruptcy and insolvency are still not discussed. The period it takes to resolve the insolvency in Kuwait is around four years or more (Raghu, Pattherwala, & Tulsyan, 2013).

In 2013, the World Bank Team launched a project with the government of Kuwait to bring up regional and international standards of Commercial law and regulation in Kuwait (Ibrahim, 2013). Issues addressed by this project were corporate rehabilitation, distress resolution, debt recovery, secured transactions, financial reporting, and strengthening the judicial system (Ibrahim, 2013).

As of May 2015, the bankruptcy regime in Kuwait is governed by Articles 555 to 800 of the Kuwait Law of Commerce No. 68 of 1980 the Current Law (Lexology, 2015). As of May 2015, a "Draft Law" is under process by the Department of Legal Opinions & Legislation of Kuwait to bring its bankruptcy and insolvency legal regime closer to Chapter 11 of the United States Bankruptcy Code (Lexology, 2015). If this law is declared, Kuwait may become the first GCC country to have a bankruptcy and insolvency regime that facilitates the rehabilitation of a debt-stricken businesses versus forced liquidation. This will enable entrepreneurs and local executives to grow businesses (Lexology, 2015).

Given is a discussion on the status of various sectors in Kuwait. According to the Oxford Business Group report on Kuwait (2015), Kuwait has oil reserves the sixth largest in the world. The revenues from hydrocarbons comprise about 60% of GDP and 95% of exports (World Bank, n.d.). Kuwait faces a long-term challenge in the recent fall in oil prices, which have added to its drive for economic diversification.

The Kuwaiti construction market saw a marked rebound in 2014, with the government moving forward with key developments in several sectors. The country's oil and gas sector was a major contributor to the country's resurgence in construction projects, with oil and gas projects representing more than 60% of the $25.1bn awarded in 2014 (World Bank, n.d.). Rising investment in real estate, meanwhile, is bolstering that sector, with the total value of transactions in 2014 increasing by almost 40% in 2013 to reach $7.27bn (Oxford Business Group, 2015).

Kuwait's insurance sector had solid expansion in recent times in key areas, including Takaful (Islamic insurance) and other non-life segments, with the industry bringing in $1.04bn in gross written premiums in 2014. The industry in Kuwait is crowded, with the top five insurers controlling around 60% of revenues at the end of 2013. The Takaful segment has been active in the country since the early 1990s, and the most recent figures show that Kuwait's 11 Islamic insurers brought in 18.7% of total gross written premiums in 2012. Meanwhile, the new health care system includes plans to cover expatriates, which accounted for an estimated 69% of the population as of the end of 2014 (Oxford Business Group, 2015).

Access to the internet, via mobile devices, has sped up quickly in Kuwait since the government liberalized the telecoms and IT sector in the early 2000s. The nation has one of the highest smartphone penetration rates in the region, at 69% of the population in 2014, after seeing 40% growth on the previous year. Meanwhile, despite new challenges in cybersecurity, there is optimism in the industry surrounding the opportunities for new businesses to help protect against cyber threats (Oxford Business Group, 2015).

Kuwait's retail market continues to perform strongly, underpinned by a strong appetite for luxury products and the strong purchasing power of a young and diverse population. The value of wholesale and retail trade in Kuwait grew 22% between 2010 and 2013, reaching a value of $5.65bn (World Bank). Meanwhile, the local retail market is forecast to expand at a compound annual growth rate (CAGR) of 6.7% between 2013 and 2018 (Oxford Business Group, 2015).

In the 2013-14 academic year, the government operated 803 public schools, with a total enrollment of 360,845 pupils and a teaching staff of 60,902 (World Bank, n.d.). Reforms are designed as the demand grows to underpin the sector's role in the government's economic diversification plan are being implemented in line with Kuwait Vision 2035, the long-term strategy, to push towards a knowledge-based economy (Oxford Business Group, 2015).

Review of Literature

Financial collapse arises when debt to creditors are not working or honored with trouble by deteriorating interest or principal payments on the debt (Aasen, 2011). This collapse leads to bankruptcy is expensive, or the firm is in an inauspicious and unsafe situation due to bad decisions (Aasen, 2011). As a result, investors agonize about the costs of financial collapse reflected in the present market value of the firm (Aasen, 2011). Investors consider the potential for future distress into their evaluation of the market value (Berk, & DeMarzo, 2011). Therefore, if a possibility of bankruptcy exists, the company's present market value is bargained by the present value of potential financial collapse expenses (Berk, & DeMarzo, 2011).

Three important factors decide the current value of financial distress expenses (Berk, & DeMarzo, 2011):

- It depends on the fact that a firm cannot fulfill its debt obligations which increase with the increase in firm's liabilities in relation to its assets, besides the unpredictability of a firm's cash flow and asset values. Firms with high business risk issue less debt is more likely to be financially distressed.

- The size of the financial distress expenses depends on the existence of direct and indirect bankruptcy costs. More debt means a higher chance of default, thus increasing the expected value of the linked costs.

- The suitable discount rate for the distress expenses depends on the firm's market risk (SlideShare, 2011, Chapter 16).

The other factors that add to bankruptcies and other distressed circumstances is based on Altman and Hotchkiss (2006):

- Repetitively sick industries (e.g., agriculture and textiles) Deregulation of industries (e.g., airline, financial services, health care, energy) High real interest rates in certain time frame Worldwide rivalry

- Excess capacity within an industry

- Greater than before leveraging of corporations

- Comparatively elevated innovative business formation rates in a certain time frame (p.13).

Kumar and Kumar (2012) stated that financial ratio analysis is used by firms to make vital decisions. Meeampol, Lerskullawat, Wongsorntham, Srinammuang, Rodpetch, & Noonoi (2014) stated that bankruptcy could be an alternative when a business is failing, but should be the last option in case everything fails. Calandro (2007) stated that the fraud metric, Altman's Z-score could be a good source for analyzing the financial performance of an organization. The Z-score financial distress model has been accepted broadly for almost four decades and influential in areas such as credit risk analysis, merger and acquisition target analysis, and turnaround management (Calandro, 2007). The Zmijewski score model compares the relative information content of these to a market-based measure of the probability of bankruptcy with traditional financial analysis (Kumar, & Kumar, 2012).

Synthesis of Research

The work of Fitzpatrick (1932) showed significant curiosity on the corporate malfunction forecast. This work used financial ratios to put side-by-side efficient firms with non-efficient firms. Altman (1968) used Beaver's work (1966) to build up a function consist of five ratios. Since then, a range of failure prediction models has been proposed using different methods, for instance, multiple discriminant analysis (e.g., Deakin, 1972; Kida, 1980; Taffler, 1983), logit and probit analysis (e.g., Ohlson, 1980; Zmijewski, 1984), neural networks (e.g.,Bell, 1997; Odom & Sharda, 1990), and hazard models (e.g., Shumway, 2001).

However, the Altman Z-score model is the most commonly recognized and used model for predicting the likelihood of a financial crash by researchers, auditors, financial analysts, corporate managements etc. (Bemmann, 2005). An abundant number of studies have been documented evidence on the performance of Altman's model. Given is an assessment of some of the studies used to evaluate stock exchange performances:

- Pongsatat, Ramage, and Lawrence (2004) compared the Ohlson's Logit model and Altman's model for predicting bankruptcy of large and small firms in Thailand and concluded that both models were similar in predicting the bankruptcy pattern.

- Chung, Tan, and Holdsworth (2008) established that the Altman model outperformed other models in predicting corporate collapse one year prior to failure for 10-unsuccessful finance companies in New Zealand during 2006-2007.

- Odipo and Sitati (2008) tested whether Altman's financial misery forecast model is useful in predicting a collapse in Kenya using ten listed firms and ten delisted firms in the Nairobi Stock Exchange from 1989 to 2008, which resulted in a precise financial crash in Kenya.

- Charles and Goodluck (2009) used a multivariate system using Altman's Z model to distinguish between unhealthy and healthy firms in the financial sector of Nigeria in the year 2009, and the outcome shows that Altman's model could predict financial failure of banks in Nigeria.

- Gerantonis, Vergos, and Christopoulos, (2009) examined the foretelling precision of Altman Z-score model for firms listed on the Athens Stock Exchange during 2002-2008. The result of the Z-score gave 66% accuracy of problems one year before the firm will exhibit financial problems. This rate slowly but diminishes to 52%, 39% and 20%, two years, three years, and four years to failure.

- Kpodoh (2009) tested data from the mobile communication industry in Ghana using the Altman's Z-score model. The findings of this study established the power and capability of the Z score model in predicting prominent business failure.

- Onyeiwu (2009) used the Altman's Z-score model to examine between healthy and unhealthy organizations in the manufacturing industry of Nigeria between 2005 and 2009 and concluded that Altman's model can group the crashed and non-distressed firms.

- Moghadam, Zadeh, and Fard (2010) used the original Altman and Ohlson models on Iranian listed companies from 1998 to 2005 and concluded that both models could forecast bankruptcy issue of listed companies in Iran.

- Wang and Campbell, (2010) used figures from Chinese listed companies for the period 2000–2008. Altman's original model, a variation of the original model for which the coefficients were recalculated, and a revised model, which used different variables were used to demonstrate that at the aggregate level, the revised Z-score model has a higher prediction precision compared with both Altman's initial model and the re-estimated model.

- Pitrova, (2011) applied the Alman's model to Czech firms four years prior to failure and resulted with 84% accuracy when predicting non-failed firms. Conversely, financial difficulties only one year prior to failure can be predicted with the highest accuracy.

- Ray (2011) examined the Indian fertilizer firms using data from 2000-2007 for bankruptcy using the Altman's model. This study could identify financially troubled companies depicting inefficiencies inside the firms that could threaten their financial health.

- Diakomihalis (2012) evaluated three versions of the Altman model (2000) on 146 private sector hotels in Greece in the year 2007. The original model reported 88.2% precision rate while the third model reported 80% precision rate.

- Li (2012) tested the predictive accuracy of Altman's initial model and two re-estimated adaptations of the initial model on a sample of 70 manufacturing and non-manufacturing US firms from 2005-2012, resulting precision rate range between 75% and 100% with an average of 91.7%.

- Mohammed and Kim-Soon (2012) compared the Altman's model and current ratio in assessing the financial status of firms listed on the Malaysian Stock Exchange. The conclusion of this study discovered that both approaches are successful in differentiating financial collapse and safe firms. Conversely, significant differences are found between the approaches one year preceding to break down.

- Onofrei and Lupu (2012) tested the Altman model in the Romanian market during 2006-2010. It was astonishing to see that this model failed on the Romanian economy as the Altman's Z-score model was developed to test stable economies only showing economic instability.

- Alareeni and Branson (2013) performed a study on 71 failed and 71 safe companies in Jordan to test the precise power of Altman's model between 1989 and 2008. The outcome predicted that the Altman Z-score model is efficient for the industrial firms, but could not distinguish between service firms.

Summary of Literature Review

The researcher observed that different country scenarios present unique results respective to the economy. Although, the predictive nature of Altman Z-score model and Zmijewski model have been accurate to a certain extent in different economies around the globe. The historical information about Kuwait stock market provides an accurate understanding of its current standing. The expansion and progress of the Kuwait stock market are guarded by various factors: deficient in market makers; overseas admittance to the market is controlled to GCC- nationals; short selling is illegal; so far no facility for securities lending and borrowing is available; less information on disclosure requirements; and bail out the speculators bail out by the government

is not accessible (Hassan et al., 2003).

Chapter 3: Methodology

The research methodology used in his study was quantitative in nature using causal research design to determine the company's performance listed on the Kuwait Stock Exchange post-financial crisis of 2008. The study aimed to build a framework to further investigate the current performance level of the listed firms by potential investors. The analysis was derived from an extensive literature review covering the history of Kuwait Stock Exchange, the theory of both Altman Z-score model and Zmijewski score model, their applications worldwide on different stock exchanges, and the conclusions in the worldwide market so far.

Purpose of the Study

This study explored the current financial condition of the listed companies on the Kuwait Stock Exchange using Altman Z-score model and Zmijewski score models. The Altman Z-score model detects stress levels in listed firms in various sectors. This model is useful for successful firm acquisition by possibly profitable firms that are interested in expanding their business. The financial ratios alone were not enough to analyze whether the firms in Kuwait stock market are profitable for foreign investment. The Zmijewski score model showed which firms are headed towards bankruptcy, and which firms are doing well. At present, the firms file for insolvency in court, which takes around four years to settle. Since no bankruptcy laws exist in Kuwait at the moment, the Zmijewski score model is an eye opener to the firms to analyze their company's financial performance and operations. This model will help the firms to decide about shutting the firm's operations if they are in the loss for several years.

Research Design

The quantitative research methodology was used on the numerical data collected from the financial statements published in company annual reports and Kuwait Stock Exchange website.

As stated by Muthukumar and Sekar (2014), the Altman Z-score model is based on the balance sheet and income statement data for determining a company's financial health. The Zmijewski score uses the probability versus traditional analysis to determine the bankruptcy occurrence within two years' time.

The causal research design is used in this research to determine the performance of the listed firms after the financial crisis of 2008. A total of 206 companies is listed on the Kuwait stock market out of which 196 are explored. The insurance companies are excluded from the study, and two are subsidiaries for one of the firms. Since the listed companies of Kuwait Stock Exchange are being evaluated; the formula used is:

$Z = 6.56\ X1 + 3.26\ X2 + 6.72\ X3 + 1.05\ X4$ (for the non-manufacturing and emerging companies).

Where

- $X1$ = working capital (current assets (CA) – current liabilities (CL)) /total assets (TA) (Calandro, 2007);

- $X2$ = retained earnings (RE) /TA;

- $X3$ = earnings before interest and taxes (EBIT) /TA; and

- $X4$ = Total book equity (TE) /Total liabilities (TL)

Altman (2002) advocated that banks and insurance companies should be excluded from the testing of Z-score model (p.5, Miller, 2009). However, for the purpose of this study, only insurance companies have been excluded.

$Z = 1.2\ X1 + 1.4\ X2 + 3.3\ X3 + 0.6\ X4 + 1.0\ X5$ (for the manufacturing companies)

(Calandro, 2007),

Where

- $X1$ = working capital (current assets (CA) – current liabilities (CL)) /total assets (TA) (Calandro, 2007);

- $X2$ = retained earnings (RE) /TA;

- $X3$ = earnings before interest and taxes (EBIT) /TA;

- $X4$ = market value of equity /book value of total liabilities (TL); and

- $X5$ = sales /TA

X1-Working Capital /TA:

The formula Working capital/TA quantify the net liquid assets of the firm compared to the total capitalization (Chouhan, et al., 2014). Working capital is the difference between current assets and current liabilities (Chouhan, et al., 2014). In general, a firm experiencing regular operating losses has shrunk current assets when compared to TA (Chouhan, et al., 2014).

X2-Retained Earnings/TA:

The formula Retained Earnings/TA evaluation of cumulative profitability was cited earlier as one of the "new" ratios (Chouhan, et al., 2014). The age of a firm is absolutely considered in this ratio (Chouhan, et al., 2014). For example, a young firm will show a low RE/TA ratio because it has not had time to build up its collective profits (Chouhan, et al., 2014). The incidence of failure is much higher in a younger firm (Chouhan, et al., 2014).

X3-EBIT/TA:

The formula Earnings before Interest and Taxes/TA is calculated by dividing the TA of a firm into its EBIT (Chouhan, et al., 2014). This measures the productivity of the firm's assets, before tax or leverage (Chouhan, et al., 2014). When the TL exceeds a fair valuation of the firm's assets, then bankruptcy occurs (Chouhan, et al., 2014).

X4-Market Value of Equity/Book Value of Total Debt:

Equity is the collective market value of all shares of stock, preferred and common while debt includes TL (Chouhan, et al., 2014). This shows how much of the firm's assets decline in value before the TL exceed the assets and the firm becomes bankrupt (Chouhan, et al., 2014). It is an efficient forecaster of bankruptcy than a used ratio: Net worth/Total debt (book values) (Chouhan, et al., 2014).

X5-Sales/TA:

This is a regular financial ratio demonstrating the sales (revenue) producing ability of the company's assets (Chouhan, et al., 2014). The management uses this formula to deal with its current competitor scenario (Chouhan, et al., 2014). Conversely, because of its exceptional relationship to other variables in the Altman model, the Sales/TA ratio ranks second in its involvement to the overall discriminating ability of the model (Chouhan, et al., 2014).

The criteria used to interpret the Z-score model is:

- Safe Zone = $Z > 2.99$ (risk free);
- Distress Zone = $Z < 1.81$ (bankruptcy); and
- Grey Zone = $1.81 <= Z <= 2.99$ (at risk) (Calandro, 2007).

For banking institutions, the Z score model formula varies from the above. Here,

Z score = 3.25 + 6.56 (X1) + 3.26 (X2) + 6.72 (X3) + 1.05 (X4),

Where X1, X2, and X3 remain same as above, and X4 = Total Book Equity (TE) /TL.

The criterion used to interpret is:

- $Z > 5.85$ Safe Zone (Aasen, 2011).
- $4.35 < Z < 5.85$ Grey Zone.
- $Z < 4.35$ Distress Zone.

Therefore, higher the score means more financially sound the company (McCallum, 2010). The Z Score Ratings used in classifying are AAA 8.15; AA 7.30; A 6.65; BBB 5.85; BB 4.95; B 4.15; CCC 3.20; and D 3.19 (McCallum, 2010).

The Zmijewski score model predicts a firm's bankruptcy in two years (YCHARTS, n.d.). This model uses three explanatory variables while an Altman Z-score uses five variables (Avenhuis, 2013). Here, the scores greater than X represent a higher probability of default (YCHARTS, n.d.). Accounting researchers like Grice and Dugan (2003), frequently use Zmijewski model, founded on the 40 bankrupt and 800 non-bankrupt firms (Avenhuis, 2013). Hence, the Z score model shows the performance of the firms while Zmijewski score model predicts whether the firm is headed towards bankruptcy.

Zmijewski Score = - 4.336 - 4.513 * (Net Income (NI) /TA) + 5.679 * (TL/TA) + 0.004 * (Current Assets (CA) /Current Liabilities (CL)) (YCHARTS, n.d.).

Firms with probabilities > = 0.5 states bankruptcy or complete data (Avenhuis, 2013);

Firms with probabilities < 0.5 states non-bankruptcy or incomplete data.

The probit model of Zmijewski is preferred because it maps the value to a probability enclosed between 0 and 1, which is straightforward to understand (Avenhuis, 2013). Firms with negative shareholder's equity, NI, and cash flow ratio are categorized as distressed and positive shareholder's equity, NI, and cash flow ratio are categorized as non-distressed (Waqas, et al., 2014). As of 2015, no bankruptcy laws are existent in Kuwait.

Research Questions and Hypotheses

This research focuses on the following research questions and hypotheses,

R1. Are the firms listed in Kuwait stock market efficient for foreign investment using the Z-score model?"

H_{01}: The models Altman's Z-score and Zmijewski's Score do not contradict each other

H_{11}: The models Altman's Z-score and Zmijewski's Score contradict each other.

R2. Is bankruptcy likely to occur in the future Kuwait market?

H_{02}: Bankruptcy does not occur in two years if Zmijewski's Score is positive

H_{12}: Bankruptcy can occur in two years if Zmijewski's Score is negative.

Population and Sampling Strategy

The population used is all the listed firms in the Kuwait Stock Exchange. The firms are classified in the following categories: KSX15, also known as "Kuwait 15" index, Oil & Gas, Basic Materials, Industrials, Consumer Goods, Health Care, Consumer Services, Telecommunications, Utilities, Banks, Real Estate, Financial Services, Investment Instruments, Technology, and Parallel.

KSX 15

o   National Bank of Kuwait

o   Gulf Bank

o   Commercial Bank of Kuwait

o   Kuwait International Bank

o   Burgan Bank

o   Kuwait Finance House

o   Boubyan Bank

o   Kuwait Projects Co. Holding

o   Mabanee Company

o   National Industries Group (Holding)

o   Agility Public Warehousing Company

- Mobile Telecommunications Company (Zain)

- Kuwait Food Company (Americana)

- Warba Bank

- Kuwait Telecommunications Company (Viva)

Oil & Gas

- Contracting & Marine Services Company

- Safat Energy Holding Company

- Independent Petroleum Group

- National Petroleum Services Company

- The Energy House Company (Aref)

- Gulf Petroleum Investment

- Burgan Company for Well Drilling Trading & Maintenance

Basic Materials

- Kuwait Foundry Company (manufacturing)

- Boubyan Petrochemical Company

- Alkout Industrial Projects Company

- Qurain Petrochemical Industries Company

Industrials

- Kuwait Cement Company (manufacturing)

- Refrigeration Industries and Storage Company

- Gulf Cable and Electrical Industries Company (manufacturing)

- Heavy Engineering Industries and Ship Building Company

- Kuwait Portland Cement Company (manufacturing)

- Shuaiba Industrial Company (manufacturing)

- Metal & Recycling Company (manufacturing)

- Acico Industries Company

- Gulf Glass Manufacturing Company Ltd (manufacturing)

- Hilal Cement Company (manufacturing)

- Kuwait Packaging Materials Manufacturing Company (manufacturing)

- Kuwait Building Materials Manufacturing Company (manufacturing)

- National Industries Company (manufacturing)

- Equipment Holding Company

- National Consumer Holding Company

- Kuwait Gypsum Manufacturing & Trading Company (manufacturing)

- Salbookh Trading Company

- Agility Public Warehousing Company

- Educational Holding Group

- National Cleaning Company

- City Group Company

- Kuwait & Gulf Link Transport Company

- The Kuwait Company for Process Plant Construction & Contracting (KCPC)

- Humansoft Holding Company

- Nafais Holding Company

- Gulf Franchising Holding Company

- National Ranges Company

- Combined Group Contracting Company

- o Mushrif Trading & Contracting Company

- o United Projects Company

- o Alafco Aviation Lease and Finance

- o Mubarrad Transport Company

- o KGL Logistics Company K.S.C.C.

- o Sharjah Cement & Industrial Development Company (manufacturing)

- o Gulf Cement Company (manufacturing)

- o Umm Al-Qaiwain Cement Industries Company (PSC) (manufacturing)

- o Fujairah Cement Industries (manufacturing)

- o Ras Al Khaimah Company for White Cement Construction Materials (manufacturing)

- o Specialities Group Holding Company (manufacturing)

Consumer Goods

- o Kuwait Slaughter House Company

- o National Slaughterhouse Company

- o Palms Agro Production Company

- o Livestock Transport & Trading Company

- o Danah AlSafat Foodstuff Company

- o Kuwait United Poultry Company

- o Kuwait Food Company(Americana)

- o Mezzan Holding Company

Health Care

- o Safwan Trading & Contracting Company

- o Al-Mowasat Health Care Company

- o   Advanced Technology Company
- o   Yiaco Medical Company

Consumer Services

- o   Kuwait National Cinema
- o   Kuwait Hotels Company
- o   Sultan Center Food Products Group Company
- o   Kuwait Cable Vision
- o   Eyas for Higher & Technical Education
- o   IFA Hotels & Resorts Company
- o   Oula Fuel Marketing Company
- o   Kuwait Resorts Company
- o   Jazeera Airways Company
- o   Soor Fuel Marketing Company
- o   Future Kid Entertainment & Real Estate
- o   Al-Nawadi Holding Company
- o   Al Rai Media Group Company
- o   Zima Holding Company
- o   United Foodstuff Industries Group Company
- o   Kout Food Group

Telecommunications

- o   Mobile Telecommunications Company (Zain)
- o   National Mobile Telecommunications Company (Ooredoo)
- o   Hits Telecom Holding Company

- o   Kuwait Telecommunications Company (Viva)

Banks

- o   National Bank of Kuwait
- o   Gulf Bank
- o   Commercial Bank of Kuwait
- o   Al Ahli Bank of Kuwait
- o   Ahli United Bank – Al Mutahed
- o   Kuwait International Bank
- o   Boubyan Bank
- o   Burgan Bank
- o   Kuwait Finance House
- o   Ithmaar Bank (B.S.C.)
- o   Warba Bank
- o   Ahli United Bank B.S.C.

Real Estate

- o   Sokouk Holding Company
- o   Kuwait Real Estate Company
- o   United Real Estate Company
- o   The National Real Estate Company
- o   Salhia Real Estate Company
- o   Tamdeen Investment Company
- o   Tamdeen Real Estate Company
- o   Ajial Real Estate Entertainment Company

- Massaleh Real Estate Company
- Al-Arabiy Real Estate Company
- Al-Enma Real Estate Company
- Mabanee Company
- Injazzat Real Estate Development Company
- Investors Holding Group Company
- International Resorts Company
- The Commercial Real Estate Company
- Sanam Real Estate Company
- A Ayan Real Estate Company
- Aqar Real Estate Investments Company
- Kuwait Real Estate Holding Company
- AL-Mazaya Holding Company
- Al-Dar National Real Estate Company
- Al-Themar International Holding Company
- Tijara & Real Estate Investment Company
- Taameer Real Estate Investment Company
- Arkan Al-Kuwait Real Estate Company
- AlArgan International Real Estate Company
- Abyaar Real Estate Development Company
- Munshaat Real Estate Projects Company
- First Dubai for Real Estate Development
- Kuwait Business Town Real Estate Company

- o   Real Estate Asset Management Company (REAM)

- o   MENA Real Estate Company

- o   Al Mudon International Real Estate Company

- o   MARAKEZ

- o   Kuwait Remal Real Estate Company

- o   Mashaer Holding Company

Financial Services

- o   Kuwait Investment Company

- o   Commercial Facilities Company

- o   International Financial Advisors

- o   National Investments Company

- o   Kuwait Projects Company Holding

- o   Coast Investment & Development Company

- o   The Securities House Company

- o   Securities Group Company

- o   Arzan Financial Group for Financing and Investment

- o   Kuwait Financial Centre

- o   Kuwait and Middle East Financial Investment Company

- o   Al-Aman Investment Company

- o   First Investment Company

- o   Al-Mal Investment Company

- o   Gulf Investment House

- o   Aayan Leasing & Investment Company

- Bayan Investment Company
- Osoul Investment Company
- Kuwait Finance & Investment Company
- KAMCO Investment Company K.S.C (PUBLIC)
- National International Holding Company
- Housing Finance Company
- Al-Madar Finance & Investment Company
- Al -Deera Holding Company
- Al Salam Group Holding Company
- Ekttitab Holding Company
- Al Qurain Holding Company
- Al - Madina for Finance and Investment Company
- Noor Financial Investment
- Tamdeen Investment Company
- Kuwait Bahrain International Exchange Company
- Taiba Kuwaiti Holding Company
- Kuwait Syrial Holding Company
- Strategia Investment Company
- Asiya Capital Investment Company
- Manafae Holding Company
- Gulf North Africa Holding Company
- Amwal International Investment Company
- AlImtiaz Investment Group Company

- o   Manazel Holding Company

- o   National Industries Group (HOLDING)

- o   Boubyan International Industries Holding Company

- o   Arabi Holding Group Company

- o   Privatization Holding Company

- o   Credit Rating & Collection

- o   Jeeran Holding Company

- o   Egypt Kuwait Holding (S.A.E)

- o   GFH Financial Group (B.S.C)

- o   Inovest (B.S.C)

Technology

- o   Automated Systems Company

- o   Future Communications Company Global

- o   Hayat Communications Company

- o   Al-Safat Tec Holding Company

Parallel

- o   Al-Bareeq Holding Company

- o   Afaq Educational Services Company

- o   AlShamel International Holding Company

- o   Al Safat Real Estate Company

- o   Ajwan Gulf Real Estate Company

- o   Dalqan Real Estate Company

- o   Al Eid Food Company

- o   Kuwait Medical Services Company

- o   Dar Al Thuraya Real Estate Company

- o   Amar for Finance & Leasing Company

- o   Flex Resorts & Real Estate Company

- o   Al Masaken International Real Estate Development Company

- o   Al-Maidan Clinic for Oral Health Services Company

The website Dissertation India states, "A sample lies between these two extremes, with between 30 and 400 respondents being a part of the study". Delice (2010) suggests that "Causal-comparative and experimental studies require more than 50 samples". Since the quantitative methodology is used, the sample used for investigation is 196 companies listed in various sectors in the Kuwait Stock Exchange.

Research Instrument

The researcher used the original Altman Z-score model for exploring the financial performance of the listed firms. However, for banks, the revised model of Altman's Z-score was used. Zmijewski score model was used to distinguish between distressed and non-distressed firms using the criterion:

Zmijewski Score < 0 shows distressed; and

Zmijewski score > 0 shows non-distress.

Currently, no bankruptcy laws are existent in Kuwait. Hence, the probit model of Zmijewski i.e. it maps the value to a probability enclosed between 0 and 1 is not applicable here.

Instrument Validation

Validity is an essential contemplation in developing and evaluating tests (Park, 2012). According to the Standards for Educational and Psychological Testing (2002), validity "refers to the degree to which evidence and theory support the interpretations of test scores entailed by proposed uses of tests" (Park, 2012,p.54). Cronbach (1971) defined validity as "the accuracy of all the analysis of a test."(p.55). All of the above definitions relate validity to the suitability of the implications included in test score interpretations. Sireci (2007) explained the fundamental aspects of validity:

• Validity refers to the use of a test for a particular rationale (Park, 2012).

• Evaluating the usefulness and suitability of a test for a particular rationale requires several sources of proof.

• Adequate proof must be put ahead to defend the use of the test for that purpose.

• Evaluating test validity is a nonstop procedure.

Following this idea, this research discovers each resource of validity proof. The sources of validity proof identified are described as follows.

Predictive/criterion validity is applicable in this research. This measures the extent to which a tool can predict a future event of interest, i.e., the financial soundness of the firm or bankruptcy occurrence this is research. Both models, i.e., Altman Z-score and Zmijewski scores are validated by testing them on the sample of 196 companies to match the criterion scale mentioned.

Data Collection Procedures

Resources and data needed for this research are secondary and gathered using the annual reports from the company websites and financial reports available on the Kuwait Stock Exchange website for the period 2009-2014. The purpose of choosing, this time frame, was to study the market after the financial crisis of 2008. Therefore, the researcher fulfilled the content validity criterion.

46

Data Analyses

The quantitative method uses the data collected to calculate both Altman Z-score and Zmijewski score for the listed firms. These two sets of data scores will be tallied with the criterion scales for each of the models to predict their performance. This will be represented using annual pie charts to understand the status of the market in Kuwait.

Summary of Methodology

The quantitative methodology uses the financial data from the annual reports of the listed companies' websites and financial reports from the Kuwait Stock Exchange website for the application of Altman Z-score model and Zmijewski score model. Both of them predict the performance and bankruptcy rate of the two sets of data using the predefined criterion scales for each of the models. The subsequent chapter will dig into further details.

Chapter 4: Analysis and Presentation of Results

In this chapter, the data was gathered from the financial statements from the annual reports and Kuwait Stock Exchange website in relation to the research questions posed in chapter 1 of this academic paper. This chapter discusses the result of the performance of the listed firms in the Kuwait Stock Exchange. Two models, Altman Z-score and Zmijewski score, were used to predict the financial status and future of the listed firms in Kuwait. To simplify the discussions, the researcher provided tables and pie charts that provide answers to the posed research questions and hypotheses mentioned in the previous chapters.

Demographic Statistics

Tables 1 and 2 show a comparison of the calculations using Altman Z-score and Zmijewski score formulae on the listed firms of Kuwait Stock Exchange from 2009-2014. The majority of the firms in the Kuwait Stock Exchange, for the years 2009 and 2010, show no data available. The Altman's Z-score model represents the following: distress level less than 1.81 for companies, and less than 4.35 for banks (55 firms by 2014), safe level greater than 2.99 for companies, and greater than 5.85 for banks (106 firms by 2014), and the neither safe nor distress level between 1.81-2.99 for companies, and between 4.35-5.85 for banks (34 firms by 2014). On the contrary, the Zmijewski score model represents the following: most distressed less than zero (148 firms by 2014), safe or non-distressed greater than zero (19 firms by 2014), and the least distressed less than negative one (28 firms by 2014).

Table 1

Altman Z-score calculations on the listed firms

Serial No.	Company Name	2009	2010	2011	2012	2013	2014
1	Aayan Real Estate Co.			3.07	3.97	6.06	5.66
2	Aayan Leasing & Investment			-4.50	-3.64	-1.94	-2.44

	Co.						
3	Al Ahli Bank of Kuwait	3.82	4.51	4.56	4.28	3.96	3.18
4	Abyaar Real Estate Development Co.	-1.66	-0.48	-0.13	-0.67	-0.61	-0.69
5	Acico Industries Co.	1.54	2.42	1.66	2.24	2.32	1.58
6	Advanced Technology Co.		2.88	3.01	2.32	2.73	3.15
7	Afaq Educational Services Co.			6.51	6.72	7.04	7.53
8	Agility Public Warehousing Co.	4.17	3.51	3.83	3.76	3.92	3.51
9	Ahli United Bank- Al Mutahed	9.80	9.91	9.93	9.93	9.92	9.93
10	Ahli United Bank B.S.C.	3.49	3.54	4.43	4.48	4.87	4.81
11	Ajial Real Estate Entertainment Co.			1.57	11.12	12.18	7.89
12	Ajwan Gulf Real Estate Co.			163.32	206.09	503.32	645.20
13	Al Eid Food Co.			6.30	6.64	6.83	6.93
14	Al Masaken International Real Estate Development Co.			11.46	7.78	3.88	2.48
15	Al Mudon International Real Estate Co.			17.22	32.01	6.27	20.84
16	Al Qurain Holding Co.			1.50	-6.29	-2.31	-1.36
17	Al Safat Real Estate Co.				-3.94	-5.77	-4.33
18	Alafco Aviation Lease and Finance	0.51	0.39	1.02	1.15	1.03	1.38
19	Al-Aman Investment Co.			0.43	2.16	3.49	38.19
20	Al-Arabiy Real Estate Co.	-1.85	-1.55	1.78	1.82	1.55	1.66
21	Alargan International Real Estate Co.	2.21	2.22	3.12	3.91	3.65	3.62
22	Al-Bareeq Holding Co.			41.04	49.52	44.21	95.19
23	Al-Dar National Real Estate Co.			-1.44	-1.75	-1.89	-1.59
24	Al-Deera Holding Co.	-0.66	-0.95	-0.72	-1.63	-1.07	-1.97
25	Al-Enmaa Real Estate Co.	1.78	1.53	3.07	2.72	2.93	2.81
26	AlImtiaz Investment Group Co.	-0.42	4.33	5.19	3.68	1.60	3.94
27	AlKout Industrial Projects Co.	4.18	6.83	5.41	4.86	5.58	9.03
28	Al-Madar Finance and Investment Co.	-0.61	-3.47	-1.95	-3.55	-1.60	-2.89
29	Al-Madina for Finance and Investment Co.			0.98	0.61	-0.05	-0.64
30	Al-Maidan Clinic for Oral Health Services Co.		-4.75	-5.42	-5.86	-3.65	-2.35
31	Al-Mal Investment Co.			-1.06	0.13	-0.07	1.06
32	Al-Mazaya Holding Co.	2.52	1.14	0.15	1.54	1.74	1.86
33	Al-Mowasat Health Care Co.			2.55	2.93	3.19	2.43
34	Al-Nawadi Holding Co.		4.57	2.67	1.57	-1.21	-0.95
35	AlRai Media Group Co.			1.58	2.47	3.86	5.71

36	Al-Safat Tec Holding Co.	4.58	3.83	1.68	2.92	1.28	0.94
37	AlSalam Group Holding Co.			6.67	16.83	11.77	15.60
38	AlShamel International Holding Co.			6.90	9.87	8.62	5.22
39	Al-Themar International Holding Co.		2.03	2.53	2.17	2.28	2.94
40	Amar for Finance and Leasing Co.	3.17	5.70	4.28	5.33	7.15	11.96
41	Amwal International Investment Co.	50.97	24.90	61.75	93.40	90.38	34.17
42	Aqar Real Estate Investments Co.	8.02	9.37	7.26	54.53	58.07	29.30
43	Arabi Holding Group Co.			1.61	2.08	2.09	4.22
44	Arkan Al-Kuwait Real Estate Co.			2.51	3.22	2.00	3.86
45	Arzan Financial Group for Financing and Investment			3.31	5.58	4.17	4.91
46	Asiya Capital Investment Co.			9.39	12.52	11.27	5.70
47	Automated Systems Co.			10.91	13.65	11.58	10.92
48	Bayan Investment Co.	2.91	3.03	2.24	1.99	2.18	3.47
49	Boubyan Bank	5.11	5.53	5.36	5.40	5.11	5.15
50	Boubyan International Industries Holding Co.			5.31	4.74	15.12	13.59
51	Boubyan Petrochemical Co.	7.82	2.56	2.39	4.37	4.74	5.16
52	Burgan Bank	5.63	5.89	6.13	5.53	5.55	5.54
53	Burgan Co. for Well Drilling Trading & Maint.		-0.52	-0.94	0.21	0.77	-0.09
54	City Group Co.	6.03	2.61	2.15	5.68	6.72	8.62
55	Coast Investment & Development Co.			3.61	3.51	3.29	4.29
56	Combined Group Contracting Co.	3.84	4.48	3.36	2.93	2.33	1.70
57	Commercial Bank of Kuwait	5.03	5.20	5.48	4.86	5.58	6.06
58	Commercial Facilities Co.	2.36	2.81	2.77	2.53	2.24	2.19
59	Contracting & Marine Services Co.			0.59	0.58	-0.11	0.08
60	Credit Rating & Collection			133.06	28.25	34.60	46.00
61	Dalaqan Real Estate Co.			177.75	152.87	86.87	71.14
62	Danah AlSafat Foodstuff Co.	14.04	14.55	4.80	2.60	2.60	3.02
63	Dar Al Thuraya Real Estate Co.			16.72	16.34	10.36	3.11
64	Educational Holding Group	0.25	0.66	-0.33	1.55	2.77	3.45
65	Egypt Kuwait Holding (S.A.E)	0.65	0.95	5.86	5.47	5.43	6.02
66	Ekttitab Holding Co.			2.12	3.65	4.63	10.87
67	Equipment Holding Co.			-1.54	-1.38	1.62	1.45
68	Eyas for Higher & Technical Education			2.51	2.89	4.88	5.86
69	First Dubai for Real Estate Development			0.54	2.36	4.12	2.18

70	First Investment Co.			1.20	3.09	4.40	3.70
71	Flex Resorts & Real Estate Co.			23.44	11.04	6.88	4.97
72	Fujairah Cement Industries			0.48	0.87	0.76	0.88
73	Future Communications Co. Global			9.37	8.81	8.61	8.15
74	Future Kid Entertainment & Real Estate			6.79	8.17	11.36	15.64
75	Gulf Bank	5.08	5.16	3.59	3.81	5.08	5.02
76	Gulf Cable and Electrical Industries Co.	2.44	3.32	4.31	3.20	2.34	2.07
77	Gulf Cement Co.			4.78	4.29	3.46	3.00
78	GFH Financial Group (B.S.C)	0.20	-5.63	-3.15	-1.14	0.37	4.77
79	Gulf Franchising Holding Co.			-4.62	2.58	2.71	2.90
80	Gulf Glass Manufacturing Co. Ltd			20.63	12.19	12.72	8.39
81	Gulf Investment House	-1.60	-3.79	-5.74	-4.44	-5.23	-4.02
82	Gulf North Africa Holding Co.	31.47	47.30	90.08	17.34	15.81	8.32
83	Gulf Petroleum Investment			0.62	0.67	1.81	1.51
84	Hayat Communications Co.			3.84	3.62	4.08	4.73
85	Heavy Engineering Industrise and Ship Building Co.	0.81	1.56	1.08	0.95	1.27	1.34
86	Hilal Cement Co.			3.48	3.04	3.29	2.31
87	Hits Telecom Holding Co.	2.18	1.30	0.76	-0.78	2.17	6.21
88	Housing Finance Co.	-2.22	-1.90	-1.27	-2.06	-1.44	-1.63
89	Humansoft Holding Co.			2.96	2.77	3.21	3.92
90	IFA Hotels & Resorts Co.	1.20	-0.68	-0.56	-1.12	-0.32	-1.78
91	Independent Petroleum Group	1.14	1.09	0.33	0.76	0.90	0.82
92	Injazzat Real Estate Development Co.	0.27	1.22	0.49	1.28	1.91	1.86
93	Inovest (B.S.C)	0.86	0.37	1.18	0.76	1.34	1.84
94	International Financial Advisors		1.00	1.98	1.84	1.91	1.63
95	International Resorts Co.			1.37	2.72	3.45	4.23
96	Investors Holding Group Co.			-8.17	-5.47	-6.12	-1.92
97	Ithmaar Bank (B.S.C)	3.09	4.41	4.41	4.44	4.40	4.21
98	Jazeera Airways Co.	-2.11	-1.39	-0.24	1.03	1.69	-1.58
99	Jeeran Holding Co.	3.30	2.61	1.32	1.70	1.71	2.99
100	KAMCO Investment Co. K.S.C (PUBLIC)	2.27	2.38	2.10	0.37	1.79	2.15
101	KGL Logistics Co. K.S.C.C.			4.89	8.65	11.21	7.78
102	Kout Food Group			5.30	5.74	4.54	4.44
103	Kuwait & Gulf Link Transport Co.	0.43	0.47	-0.65	-1.05	0.94	0.91
104	Kuwait and Middle East Financial Investment Co.	2.85	2.08	-0.03	1.26	1.48	2.00

105	Kuwait Bahrain International Exchange Co.		8.36	8.06	8.88	9.27	10.32
106	Kuwait Building Materials Manufacturing Co.			3.37	3.46	6.68	9.14
107	Kuwait Business Town Real Estate Co.			-0.44	-1.13	5.39	8.36
108	Kuwait Cable Vision			-9.94	-11.47	-3.45	-3.73
109	Kuwait Cement Co.		2.99	2.02	1.84	1.91	2.11
110	Kuwait Finance & Investment Co.		-2.74	-1.43	5.95	5.82	5.80
111	Kuwait Finance House	7.37	7.06	7.48	7.45	7.58	7.43
112	Kuwait Financial Centre	5.26	5.35	3.31	3.89	4.64	3.36
113	Kuwait Food Co.(AMERICANA)			3.48	3.63	3.96	4.06
114	Kuwait Foundry Co.			16.81	19.89	21.73	17.04
115	Kuwait Gypsum Manufacturing & Trading Co.		3.47	2.67	3.60	4.76	6.27
116	Kuwait Hotels Co.			-0.39	0.84	1.14	1.18
117	Kuwait International Bank	7.90	8.09	8.04	8.12	8.12	7.85
118	Kuwait Investment Co.	6.13	6.80	2.18	2.69	3.42	2.67
119	Kuwait Medical Services Co.		2.34		0.71	-0.61	-1.40
120	Kuwait National Cinema	2.15	2.20	1.84	2.85	4.24	3.94
121	Kuwait Packing Materials Manufacturing Co.		8.29	7.10	8.73	8.46	6.42
122	Kuwait Portland Cement Co.	8.47	11.11	10.29	9.05	11.24	5.84
123	Kuwait Projects Co. Holding			4.93	4.79	4.83	4.89
124	Kuwait Real Estate Co.			1.85	1.89	2.28	1.40
125	Kuwait Real Estate Holding Co.			-2.27	-0.60	-2.26	-0.67
126	Kuwait Remal Real Estate Co.		2.09	2.42	2.23	2.84	2.47
127	Kuwait Resorts Co.			0.24	0.10	2.49	2.57
128	Kuwait Slaughter House Co.		30.52	21.01	23.85	21.45	23.83
129	Kuwait Syrian Holding Co.			6.38	4.24	11.95	58.00
130	Kuwait Telecommunications Co.- VIVA	-7.15	-7.40	-6.13	-6.21	-3.27	0.20
131	Kuwait United Poultry Co.			6.68	6.77	10.31	11.05
132	Livestock Transport & Trading Co.	15.89	12.12	10.81	10.27	9.60	8.10
133	Mabanee Co.	0.30	1.62	1.33	1.52	2.58	1.69
134	Manafae Holding Co.			42.16	25.81	29.51	31.24
135	Manazel Holding Co.			-1.46	-1.79	2.53	4.54
136	Marakez			1.45	1.39	1.28	1.44
137	Mashaer Holding Co.	1.41	-1.69	1.50	1.90	4.33	1.99
138	Massaleh Real Estate Co.			0.87	0.51	-0.46	-0.31
139	MENA Real Estate Co.			1.38	0.82	-0.96	1.46

140	Metal & Recycling Co.			2.45	2.54	2.62	1.70
141	Mezzan Holding Co.			3.43	2.96	3.25	3.15
142	Mobile Telecommunications Co. - ZAIN	0.56	5.32	2.75	1.90	2.13	1.69
143	Mubarrad Transport Co.			4.69	-1.12	8.82	7.33
144	Munshaat Real Estate Projects Co.	-2.82	-4.03	-3.09	-1.35	1.95	2.18
145	Mushrif Trading & Contracting Co.			2.76	3.23	3.30	2.20
146	Nafais Holding Co.			0.52	1.63	2.84	5.98
147	National Bank of Kuwait	5.20	5.13	5.35	5.57	5.45	5.69
148	National Cleaning Co.			3.59	1.69	2.23	2.14
149	National Consumer Holding Co.			18.93	17.02	8.70	5.38
150	National Industries Co.			4.13	4.33	4.66	7.17
151	National Industries Group(Holding) (Comprises of NOOR,IKARUS Petroleum,NIC, and NIG subsidiaries)			0.05	0.33	0.39	0.52
152	National International Holding Co.			7.13	5.43	21.46	19.53
153	National Investments Co.	8.54	9.38	6.75	30.17	28.88	16.00
154	National Petroleum Services Co.	5.29	5.96	6.67	8.10	7.26	7.69
155	National Ranges Co.			-2.76	-0.14	-0.32	-4.00
156	National Slaughterhouse Co.			27.29	28.08	23.00	20.36
157	Noor Financial Investment	-0.03	-0.01	0.70	1.57	1.88	1.46
158	National Mobile Telecommunications Co. - OOREDOO			4.12	2.68	1.73	1.30
159	Osoul Investment Co.			5.76	13.45	18.36	19.30
160	Oula Fuel Marketing Co.	5.91	5.90	5.10	5.57	6.16	5.05
161	Palms Agro Production Co.	10.99	9.18	8.45	6.70	7.35	8.11
162	Privatization Holding Co.			0.97	2.07	0.70	3.49
163	Qurain Petrochemical Industries Co.	16.12	115.65	83.23		44.28	7.03
164	Ras Al Khaimah Co. for White Cement Construction Materials			2.88	2.07	1.77	1.72
165	Real Estate Asset Management Co. (REAM)	10.11	9.76	10.40	10.22	3.02	6.34
166	Refrigeration Industries and Storage Co.			4.20	6.13	5.20	5.17
167	Safat Energy Holding Co.		7.61	4.08	6.86	6.24	-2.84
168	Safwan Trading & Contracting Co.			3.33	3.31	2.63	2.53
169	Salbookh Trading Co.			-0.65	2.91	4.37	6.78
170	Salhia Real Estate Co.	2.84	2.55	3.18	3.20	3.64	3.37
171	Sanam Real Estate Co.			8.60	105.88	84.78	90.07

172	Securities Group Co.		2.45	2.03	3.17	1.52	2.96
173	Sharjah Cement & Industrial Development Co.	2.00	1.45	0.87	1.29		
174	Shuaiba Industrial Co.			3.17	3.49	4.46	4.63
175	Sokouk Holding Co.	68.05	4.33	3.43	6.02	6.68	5.84
176	Soor Fuel Marketing Co.	8.16	7.21	5.75	6.02	6.30	5.42
177	Specialities Group Holding Co.	4.47	3.75	3.64	5.97	4.54	3.32
178	Strategia Investment Co.	-3.87	6.29	56.69	70.87	12.12	81.01
179	Sultan Center Food Products Group Co.	-1.63	-3.71	-5.29	-4.05	-3.92	-2.41
180	Taameer Real Estate Investment Co.			8.05	8.21	6.57	4.44
181	Taiba Kuwaiti Holding Co.			9.29	90.20	6.73	6.48
182	Tamdeen Investment Co.	1.83	2.44	3.47	3.38	3.86	1.69
183	Tamdeen Real Estate Co.			1.53	1.24	1.33	1.03
184	The Commercial Real Estate Co.			3.82	3.74	3.44	3.20
185	The Energy House Co.-AREF	3.18	7.45	5.59	3.02	6.43	8.51
186	The Kuwait Co. for Process Plant Construction & Contracting - KCPC			2.39	2.55	1.55	2.24
187	The National Real Estate Co.		0.35	-0.65	-0.17	-0.06	-0.02
188	The Securities House Co.			3.01	1.22	0.98	0.74
189	Tijaria & Real Estate Investment Co.			0.23	0.72	2.93	2.84
190	Umm Al-Qaiwain Cement Industries Co. (PSC)			4.99	5.57	5.67	5.08
191	United Foodstuff Industries Group Co.			2.53	3.27	-0.76	2.09
192	United Projects Co.	4.78	6.27	6.32	7.96	6.03	6.16
193	United Real Estate Co.	1.10	2.53	2.05	1.53	2.07	2.58
194	Warba Bank			8.68	7.13	8.29	8.32
195	Yiaco Medical Co.	2.01	2.61	2.66	2.67	2.41	2.33
196	Zima Holding Co.			4.43	5.68	9.28	5.80
	Total	401.41	507.47	1498.51	1613.22	1783.01	1999.10
	Mean	5.02	5.23	7.72	8.27	9.14	10.25
	Standard Deviation	10.22	13.19	22.35	22.81	37.73	47.60

Table 2

Zmijewski score calculations on the listed firms

Serial No.	Company Name	2009	2010	2011	2012	2013	2014
1	Aayan Real Estate Co.			-1.95	-2.58	-2.72	-2.92

2	Aayan Leasing & Investment Co.			1.10	0.37	-0.65	-0.65
3	Al Ahli Bank of Kuwait	0.65	0.37	0.37	0.32	0.34	0.39
4	Abyaar Real Estate Development Co.	-0.42	-0.69	-0.88	-1.15	-1.19	-1.48
5	Acico Industries Co.	-4.40	-0.66	-0.63	-0.66	-0.79	-0.62
6	Advanced Technology Co.		-1.09	-1.03	-0.98	-0.99	-0.91
7	Afaq Educational Services Co.			-3.54	-3.59	-3.59	-3.62
8	Agility Public Warehousing Co.	-2.08	-2.23	-2.40	-2.39	-2.43	-2.37
9	Ahli United Bank- Al Mutahed	0.97	0.91	0.95	0.89	0.95	1.05
10	Ahli United Bank B.S.C.	-2.89	-2.92	0.72	0.69	0.66	0.64
11	Ajial Real Estate Entertainment Co.			-2.18	-3.75	-3.85	-3.61
12	Ajwan Gulf Real Estate Co.			-3.91	-4.08	-2.72	-1.69
13	Al Eid Food Co.			-2.29	-2.31	-2.50	-2.50
14	Al Masaken International Real Estate Development Co.			-3.47	-3.57	-3.00	-2.68
15	Al Mudon International Real Estate Co.			-4.01	-0.32	-3.69	-4.18
16	Al Qurain Holding Co.			-2.25	0.16	-2.62	-3.17
17	Al Safat Real Estate Co.				0.66	-0.07	-0.34
18	Alafco Aviation Lease and Finance	-0.13	0.17	-0.41	-0.45	-0.33	-0.46
19	Al-Aman Investment Co.			-0.84	-0.70	-1.31	-4.88
20	Al-Arabiy Real Estate Co.	-0.83	-1.03	-0.87	-0.97	-0.80	-0.86
21	Alargan International Real Estate Co.	-2.08	-2.14	-2.16	-1.90	-1.62	-1.66
22	Al-Bareeq Holding Co.			-3.90	-4.14	-4.27	-4.17
23	Al-Dar National Real Estate Co.			0.28	0.61	0.69	0.46
24	Al-Deera Holding Co.	-1.74	-1.98	-1.00	-0.24	-0.96	-0.20
25	Al-Enmaa Real Estate Co.	-2.19	-2.46	-2.41	-2.17	-2.15	-2.08
26	AlImtiaz Investment Group Co.	-0.42	-2.72	-3.01	-2.32	-1.57	-2.73
27	AlKout Industrial Projects Co.	-2.51	-3.60	-3.20	-3.22	-3.68	-4.27
28	Al-Madar Finance and Investment Co.	-0.06	0.75	-0.71	0.21	-1.42	-0.97
29	Al-Madina for Finance and Investment Co.			-1.44	-1.48	-0.79	-0.53
30	Al-Maidan Clinic for Oral Health Services Co.		0.59	0.84	1.08	-0.37	-1.04
31	Al-Mal Investment Co.			-0.06	-0.71	-0.22	-1.02
32	Al-Mazaya Holding Co.	-1.32	-0.61	-0.33	-0.91	-1.19	-1.13
33	Al-Mowasat Health Care Co.			-1.29	-1.53	-1.61	-2.41
34	Al-Nawadi Holding Co.		-3.31	-3.08	-2.80	-1.73	-1.96

35	AlRai Media Group Co.			-2.18	-2.70	-3.36	-3.52
36	Al-Safat Tec Holding Co.	-2.78	-2.36	-1.65	-2.20	-1.24	-1.80
37	AlSalam Group Holding Co.			-3.90	-4.31	-3.83	-4.16
38	AlShamel International Holding Co.			-2.85	-3.58	-3.62	-1.87
39	Al-Themar International Holding Co.		-2.09	-2.35	-2.05	-2.09	-2.56
40	Amar for Finance and Leasing Co.	-1.56	-2.67	-2.86	-3.13	-3.78	-3.90
41	Amwal International Investment Co.	-4.21	-2.55	-4.01	-3.58	-4.02	-4.00
42	Aqar Real Estate Investments Co.	-3.15	-3.49	-3.24	-4.58	-4.53	-4.07
43	Arabi Holding Group Co.			-0.60	-0.46	0.21	0.49
44	Arkan Al-Kuwait Real Estate Co.			-2.86	-2.67	-2.54	-3.38
45	Arzan Financial Group for Financing and Investment			1.59	-3.41	-3.28	-3.55
46	Asiya Capital Investment Co.			-3.35	-4.11	-3.88	-3.56
47	Automated Systems Co.			-3.61	-4.75	-3.85	-3.73
48	Bayan Investment Co.	-0.58	-0.59	-0.92	-0.76	-1.14	-1.89
49	Boubyan Bank	1.20	0.41	0.50	0.64	0.70	0.73
50	Boubyan International Industries Holding Co.			-3.03	-2.37	-3.24	-3.44
51	Boubyan Petrochemical Co.	-1.99	-2.10	-2.33	-2.61	-2.79	-3.11
52	Burgan Bank	0.76	0.64	0.64	0.75	0.88	0.65
53	Burgan Co. for Well Drilling Trading & Maint.		-0.62	-0.42	-0.58	-0.73	-0.82
54	City Group Co.	-3.59	-2.33	-1.70	-3.40	-3.74	-4.13
55	Coast Investment Development Co.			-1.11	-1.19	-1.59	-2.16
56	Combined Group Contracting Co.	-0.50	-0.47	-4.31	-0.38	-0.01	0.14
57	Commercial Bank of Kuwait	0.66	0.55	0.64	0.50	0.60	0.61
58	Commercial Facilities Co.	-1.51	-1.98	-1.88	-4.26	-2.18	-2.01
59	Contracting & Marine Services Co.			-1.30	-1.41	-1.12	-0.81
60	Credit Rating & Collection			-3.20	-3.02	-3.65	-3.17
61	Dalaqan Real Estate Co.			-4.07	-4.29	-3.99	-2.92
62	Danah AlSafat Foodstuff Co.	-4.14	-4.10	-2.99	-2.34	-2.57	-2.94
63	Dar Al Thuraya Real Estate Co.			-4.29	-4.51	-4.10	-3.02
64	Educational Holding Group	-0.82	-1.36	-1.80	-1.90	-2.40	-2.64
65	Egypt Kuwait Holding (S.A.E)	-3.72	-3.83	-2.23	-1.92	-1.92	-2.23
66	Ekttitab Holding Co.			-2.40	-3.09	-3.19	-3.48
67	Equipment Holding Co.			-0.56	-0.60	-2.17	-2.14
68	Eyas for Higher & Technical Education			-2.29	-2.45	-3.46	-3.61

69	First Dubai for Real Estate Development			-1.97	-3.08	-3.66	-2.53
70	First Investment Co.			-2.54	-3.11	-3.11	-3.13
71	Flex Resorts & Real Estate Co.			-4.12	-3.89	-2.40	-3.31
72	Fujairah Cement Industries			-1.34	-1.74	-1.68	-1.84
73	Future Communications Co. Global			-3.25	-3.04	-3.07	-2.96
74	Future Kid Entertainment & Real Estate			-3.69	-3.79	-3.98	-4.07
75	Gulf Bank	0.91	0.85	0.81	0.80	0.80	0.81
76	Gulf Cable and Electrical Industries Co.	-2.32	-3.09	-3.56	-2.82	-2.59	-2.33
77	Gulf Cement Co.			-5.48	-5.75	-5.33	-5.33
78	GFH Financial Group (B.S.C)	1.84	2.23	-0.28	-1.15	-1.79	-2.44
79	Gulf Franchising Holding Co.			-0.59	-1.77	-1.84	-1.88
80	Gulf Glass Manufacturing Co. Ltd			-4.45	-4.43	-4.30	-4.18
81	Gulf Investment House	-0.05	0.63	0.24	-0.24	-0.18	-0.14
82	Gulf North Africa Holding Co.	-4.36	-4.18	-3.53	-2.96	-3.89	-3.50
83	Gulf Petroleum Investment			-1.76	-1.98	-2.80	-2.64
84	Hayat Communications Co.			-1.15	-1.11	-1.48	-1.90
85	Heavy Engineering Industrise and Ship Building Co.	-0.39	-0.99	-0.75	-0.40	-0.49	-0.46
86	Hilal Cement Co.			-3.19	-3.04	-2.94	-2.53
87	Hits Telecom Holding Co.	-2.55	-2.25	-2.20	-1.45	-1.97	-3.03
88	Housing Finance Co.	0.23	0.21	1.08	1.54	-0.88	-0.38
89	Humansoft Holding Co.			-2.68	-2.29	-2.65	-2.83
90	IFA Hotels & Resorts Co.	0.04	0.81	0.63	0.62	0.17	0.91
91	Independent Petroleum Group	0.11	0.05	0.47	0.07	-0.09	-0.22
92	Injazzat Real Estate Development Co.	-0.11	-0.68	-0.54	-1.29	-1.73	-1.70
93	Inovest (B.S.C)	-3.64	-3.48	-1.61	-1.84	-1.80	-2.03
94	International Financial Advisors		0.17	0.24	0.47	-0.07	0.70
95	International Resorts Co.			-1.22	-1.91	-2.02	-1.22
96	Investors Holding Group Co.			0.01	-1.80	-1.75	-1.69
97	Ithmaar Bank (B.S.C)	-3.16	-0.29	-0.47	-0.63	-0.68	-0.61
98	Jazeera Airways Co.	0.34	0.91	0.24	-0.63	-1.07	-0.28
99	Jeeran Holding Co.	-1.39	-1.10	-0.34	-0.43	-0.25	-0.33
100	KAMCO Investment Co. K.S.C (PUBLIC)	-1.86	-1.77	-1.58	-0.49	-1.86	-2.11
101	KGL Logistics Co. K.S.C.C.			-3.62	-4.23	-4.35	-3.71
102	Kout Food Group			-3.05	-3.16	-2.57	-2.53

103	Kuwait & Gulf Link Transport Co.	-0.50	-0.42	-0.17	-0.13	-0.21	-0.16
104	Kuwait and Middle East Financial Investment Co.	-1.20	-1.30	-0.21	-1.13	-1.43	-1.19
105	Kuwait Bahrain International Exchange Co.		-3.08	-3.17	-3.44	-3.51	-3.62
106	Kuwait Building Materials Manufacturing Co.			-2.98	-3.28	-3.82	-3.86
107	Kuwait Business Town Real Estate Co.			-1.04	-0.72	-3.91	-3.92
108	Kuwait Cable Vision			0.03	-1.44	-0.37	-0.83
109	Kuwait Cement Co.		-2.33	-2.14	-1.89	-2.45	-2.48
110	Kuwait Finance & Investment Co.		6.33	4.74	-2.02	-1.98	-2.30
111	Kuwait Finance House	0.32	0.38	0.46	0.44	0.60	0.63
112	Kuwait Financial Centre	-2.63	-2.82	-2.12	-3.09	-3.37	-3.08
113	Kuwait Food Co.(AMERICANA)			-2.24	-2.30	-2.31	-2.34
114	Kuwait Foundry Co.			-3.78	-4.23	-4.30	-4.31
115	Kuwait Gypsum Manufacturing & Trading Co.		-3.42	-3.35	-3.73	-3.49	-4.00
116	Kuwait Hotels Co.			-0.84	-1.37	-1.29	-1.32
117	Kuwait International Bank	0.53	0.32	0.26	0.33	0.46	0.50
118	Kuwait Investment Co.	-0.74	-1.18	-1.52	-1.45	-2.11	-2.13
119	Kuwait Medical Services Co.				-2.27	-1.76	-1.67
120	Kuwait National Cinema	-2.43	-2.61	-2.51	-2.82	-3.40	-3.37
121	Kuwait Packing Materials Manufacturing Co.		-4.00	-4.44	-4.37	-4.19	-4.02
122	Kuwait Portland Cement Co.	-4.55	-4.28	-4.06	-4.09	-4.11	-3.42
123	Kuwait Projects Co. Holding			0.37	0.52	0.64	0.59
124	Kuwait Real Estate Co.			-2.42	-2.32	-2.61	-1.99
125	Kuwait Real Estate Holding Co.			0.45	-0.13	0.68	-0.53
126	Kuwait Remal Real Estate Co.		-2.06	-2.19	-2.09	-1.89	-1.91
127	Kuwait Resorts Co.			-0.27	-0.63	-1.57	-2.07
128	Kuwait Slaughter House Co.		-4.65	-4.70	-4.86	-4.74	-4.36
129	Kuwait Syrian Holding Co.			-2.85	-2.29	-3.51	-2.71
130	Kuwait Telecommunications Co.- VIVA	1.96	2.50	2.69	1.86	0.43	-0.83
131	Kuwait United Poultry Co.			-3.94	-3.77	-4.11	-4.19
132	Livestock Transport & Trading Co.	-4.30	-3.48	-3.10	-2.98	-3.59	-3.00
133	Mabanee Co.	-1.84	-1.80	-1.67	-1.92	-2.40	-1.95
134	Manafae Holding Co.			-3.57	-3.37	-3.82	-4.22
135	Manazel Holding Co.			-0.58	-0.42	-0.98	-3.00
136	Marakez			-2.67	-2.67	-2.63	-2.71

137	Mashaer Holding Co.	-2.68	-0.34	-2.11	-2.54	-2.87	-1.91
138	Massaleh Real Estate Co.			-1.09	-0.86	-0.15	-0.15
139	MENA Real Estate Co.			-1.61	-1.94	-1.55	-2.70
140	Metal & Recycling Co.			-3.37	-3.23	-3.24	-3.26
141	Mezzan Holding Co.			-2.03	-1.95	-1.97	-2.13
142	Mobile Telecommunications Co. - ZAIN	-1.29	-3.28	-2.85	-2.36	-2.20	-2.03
143	Mubarrad Transport Co.			-3.04	-0.91	-3.72	-3.92
144	Munshaat Real Estate Projects Co.	0.71	0.65	0.94	0.03	-2.76	-2.69
145	Mushrif Trading & Contracting Co.			-0.85	-0.88	-0.52	-0.93
146	Nafais Holding Co.			-2.14	-2.40	-2.81	-3.79
147	National Bank of Kuwait	0.50	0.31	0.34	0.47	0.55	0.64
148	National Cleaning Co.			-2.41	-1.31	-1.17	-1.06
149	National Consumer Holding Co.			-2.98	-3.88	-3.45	-3.24
150	National Industries Co.			-2.99	-3.08	-3.08	-3.66
151	National Industries Group(Holding) (Comprises of NOOR,IKARUS Petroleum,NIC, and NIG subsidiaries)			-0.52	-0.84	-1.01	-1.14
152	National International Holding Co.			-3.31	-2.93	-4.24	-4.15
153	National Investments Co.	-2.61	-3.14	-3.04	-4.28	-4.26	-4.12
154	National Petroleum Services Co.	-2.86	-3.30	-3.55	-3.75	-3.67	-3.66
155	National Ranges Co.			0.18	-1.00	-1.02	-0.28
156	National Slaughterhouse Co.			-4.58	-4.49	-4.35	-4.24
157	Noor Financial Investment	-0.18	-0.29	0.18	-0.46	-0.61	-0.46
158	National Mobile Telecommunications Co. - OOREDOO			-3.46	-2.57	-2.09	-1.92
159	Osoul Investment Co.			-3.42	-3.94	-4.04	-4.07
160	Oula Fuel Marketing Co.	-3.55	-3.52	-3.33	-3.42	-3.59	-3.07
161	Palms Agro Production Co.	-3.91	-3.53	-3.34	-3.07	-3.17	-3.26
162	Privatization Holding Co.			-1.32	-2.35	-1.91	-2.10
163	Qurain Petrochemical Industries Co.	-4.11	-4.21	-4.79		-4.50	-3.83
164	Ras Al Khaimah Co. for White Cement Construction Materials			-3.30	-3.09	-2.87	-2.81
165	Real Estate Asset Management Co. (REAM)	-3.93	-3.85	-3.88	-3.90	-3.24	-3.58
166	Refrigeration Industries and Storage Co.			-2.17	-3.38	-2.81	-2.65
167	Safat Energy Holding Co.		-3.46	-2.61	-3.76	-3.06	-0.75
168	Safwan Trading & Contracting Co.			-1.00	-0.97	-0.63	-0.47

169	Salbookh Trading Co.			-1.84	-1.88	-2.57	-3.19
170	Salhia Real Estate Co.	-1.66	-2.29	-2.00	-2.17	-2.58	-2.43
171	Sanam Real Estate Co.			-2.77	-4.22	-4.26	-4.11
172	Securities Group Co.		-1.94	-1.24	-2.29	-1.06	-1.41
173	Sharjah Cement & Industrial Development Co.	-3.23	-3.05	-2.81	-2.96		
174	Shuaiba Industrial Co.			-3.53	-3.65	-3.73	-3.76
175	Sokouk Holding Co.	-2.33	-1.99	-2.51	-2.92	-3.42	-2.88
176	Soor Fuel Marketing Co.	-3.75	-3.56	-3.41	-3.48	-3.55	-3.39
177	Specialities Group Holding Co.	-3.22	-3.45	-3.45	-3.74	-3.69	-3.77
178	Strategia Investment Co.	0.84	-2.33	-4.18	-4.19	-4.13	-4.33
179	Sultan Center Food Products Group Co.	-0.60	0.41	1.18	0.52	0.51	0.52
180	Taameer Real Estate Investment Co.			-3.12	-3.35	-2.47	-1.57
181	Taiba Kuwaiti Holding Co.			-3.99	-5.10	-3.62	-3.55
182	Tamdeen Investment Co.	-1.78	-2.34	-2.49	-2.93	-3.06	-2.33
183	Tamdeen Real Estate Co.			-1.79	-1.82	-2.05	-1.77
184	The Commercial Real Estate Co.			-2.64	-2.80	-2.81	-2.71
185	The Energy House Co.- AREF	-2.00	-3.26	-2.94	-2.64	-3.64	-3.64
186	The Kuwait Co. for Process Plant Construction & Contracting - KCPC			-1.55	-1.49	-1.26	-1.92
187	The National Real Estate Co.		-0.85	-0.40	-0.42	-1.02	-1.03
188	The Securities House Co.			-2.64	-1.33	-1.37	-1.82
189	Tijaria & Real Estate Investment Co.			-0.94	-1.22	-2.91	-2.45
190	Umm Al-Qaiwain Cement Industries Co. (PSC)			-4.12	-4.08	-4.10	-3.94
191	United Foodstuff Industries Group Co.			-2.42	-2.67	-0.61	-2.29
192	United Projects Co.	-3.29	-3.53	-3.51	-4.15	-4.09	-3.81
193	United Real Estate Co.	-1.45	-1.85	-1.44	-1.51	-1.38	-1.28
194	Warba Bank			-3.08	-1.04	0.13	0.48
195	Yiaco Medical Co.	-1.01	-1.20	-1.27	-1.09	-0.85	-0.63
196	Zima Holding Co.			-2.75	-3.10	-3.49	-2.91
	Total	-124.48	-150.62	-369.79	-398.49	-426.23	-429.14
	Mean	-1.56	-1.57	-1.91	-2.04	-2.19	-2.20
	Standard Deviation	1.69	1.84	1.63	1.57	1.49	1.48

The mean in both tables shows different directions, i.e., Table 1 mean is positive, whereas, Table 2 mean is negative. However, further analysis is explained in the next section.

The sectors performing well and good for investment are banking, food, petroleum, slaughterhouses, technology, and parallel markets.

Details of Analysis and Results

Figure 1 and 2 for the year for the year 2009 illustrates that both Altman Z-score and Zmijewski score models were not in par with each other in predicting the status of the listed firms in the Kuwait Stock Exchange. Around 59.2% of the firms have no information. The Altman's Z-score model indicated 15.31% firms were safe while, Zmijewski's score model showed 8.67%. The Altman's Z-score model indicated 16.33% firms were distressed while, Zmijewski's score model showed 24.49%. Finally, the Altman's Z-score model indicated 9.18% firms were neither safe nor distressed while, Zmijewski's score model showed 7.65%. Therefore, the hypothesis H_{11}: The models Altman's Z-score and Zmijewski's Score contradict each other is true.

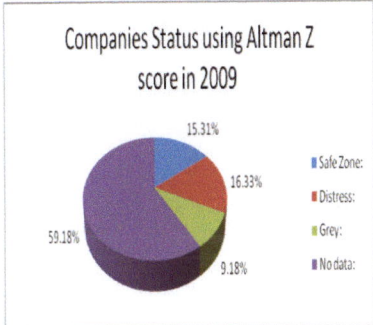

Figure 1. Companies Status of the Altman Z-score in 2009

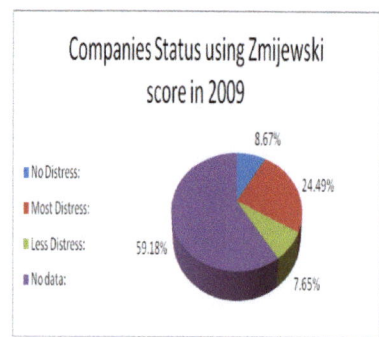

Figure 2. Companies Status of the Zmijewski score in 2009

Figure 3 and 4 for the year 2010 illustrates that both Altman Z-score and Zmijewski score models were not in par with each other. Around 50.51% of the firms have no information. The Altman's Z-score model indicated 19.90% firms were safe while, Zmijewski's score model showed 11.73%. The Altman's Z-score model indicated 16.84% firms were distressed while, Zmijewski's score model showed 30.61%. Finally, the Altman's Z-score model indicated 12.76% firms were neither safe nor distressed while, Zmijewski's score model showed 7.14%. Therefore, the hypothesis H_{1}: The models Altman's Z-score and Zmijewski's Score contradict each other is true.

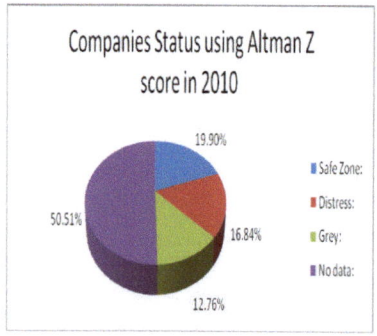

Figure 3. Companies Status of the Altman Z-score in 2010

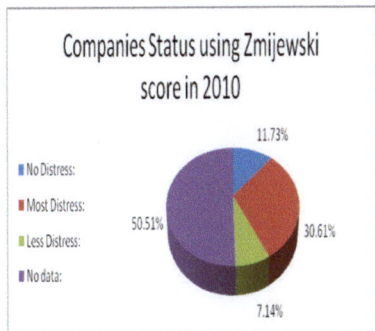

Figure 4. Companies Status of the Zmijewski score in 2010

Figure 5 and 6 for the year 2011 illustrates that both Altman Z-score and Zmijewski score models are not in agreement with each other. The Zmijewski score model shows a higher amount of distressed firms when compared to the Altman Z-score model. The Altman's Z-score model indicated 47.45% firms were safe while, Zmijewski's score model showed 15.31%. The Altman's Z-score model indicated 35.20% firms were distressed while, Zmijewski's score model showed 68.88%. Finally, the Altman's Z-score model indicated 16.33% firms were neither safe nor distressed while, Zmijewski's score model showed 14.80%. All positive ratios in Zmijewski model show a non-distressed firm and vice versa. Since, the theories behind Zmijewski model are contradictory, therefore, the hypothesis H_{1i}: The models Altman's Z-score and Zmijewski's Score contradict each other is true.

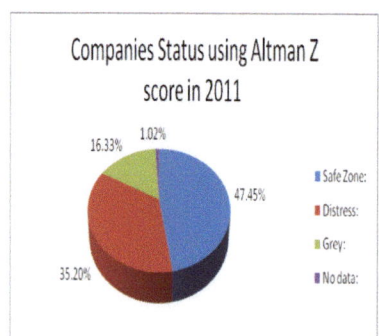

Figure 5. Companies Status of the Altman Z-score in 2011

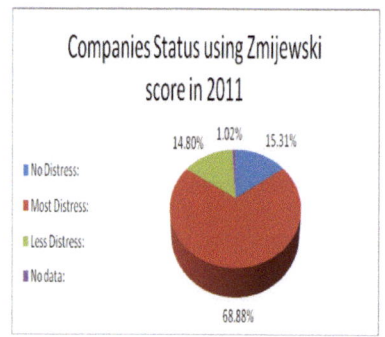

Figure 6. Companies Status of the Zmijewski score in 2011

Figure 7 and 8 for the year 2012 illustrates the same pattern as above in 2011. The

Zmijewski score model shows a greater amount of distressed firms when compared to the

Altman Z-score model. The number of firms that were financially secure are 48.47% in Altman's

Z-score model when compared to 12.24% in Zmijewski's score model. The Altman's Z-score

model indicated 32.14% firms were distressed while, Zmijewski's score model showed 70.41%.

Finally, the Altman's Z-score model indicated 18.88% firms were neither safe nor distressed

while, Zmijewski's score model showed 16.84%. All positive ratios in Zmijewski model show a non-distressed firm and vice versa. Since, the theories behind Zmijewski model are contradictory, therefore, the hypothesis H_{11}: The models Altman's Z-score and Zmijewski's Score contradict each other is true.

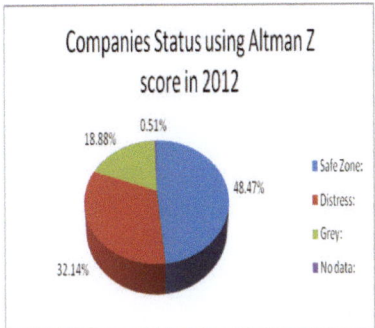

Figure 7. Companies Status of the Altman Z-score in 2012

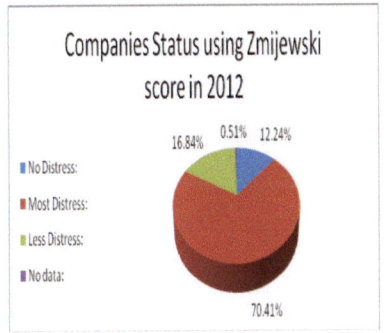

Figure 8. Companies Status of the Zmijewski score in 2012

Figure 9 and 10 for the year 2013 illustrates the same pattern as previous years, 2011 and 2012. The Zmijewski score model shows a greater amount of distressed firms when compared to the Altman Z-score model. The number of firms that were financially secure are 51.53% in Altman's Z-score model when compared to 9.69% in Zmijewski's score model. The Altman's Z-score model indicated 27.04% firms were distressed while, Zmijewski's score model showed

76.53%. Finally, the Altman's Z-score model indicated 20.92% firms were neither safe nor distressed while, Zmijewski's score model showed 13.27%. All positive ratios in Zmijewski model show a non-distressed firm and vice versa. Hence, the theories behind Zmijewski model are contradictory. Therefore, the hypothesis H_{11}: The models Altman's Z-score and Zmijewski's Score contradict each other is true.

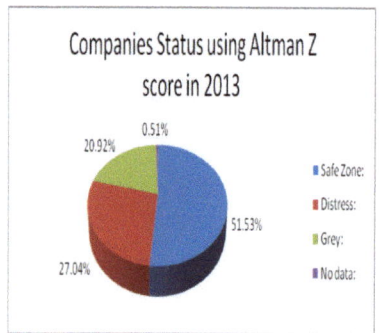

*Figure 9.*Companies Status of the Altman Z-score in 2013

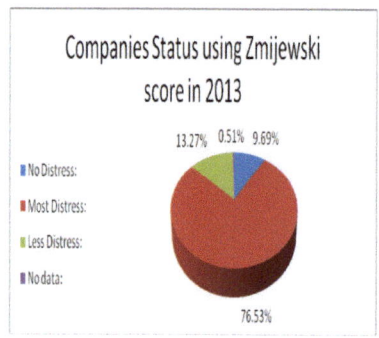

Figure 10. Companies Status of the Zmijewski score in 2013

Figure 11 and 12 for the year 2014 illustrates the same pattern as previous years, 2011, 2012, and 2013. The Zmijewski score model shows slightly lesser distressed firms when compared to 2013. The number of firms that were financially secure are 54.08% in Altman's Z-score model when compared to 9.69% in Zmijewski's score model in 2014. The Altman's Z-score model indicated 28.06% firms were distressed while, Zmijewski's score model showed 75.51%. Finally, the Altman's Z-score model indicated 17.35% firms were neither safe nor distressed while, Zmijewski's score model showed 14.29%. All positive ratios in Zmijewski model show a non-distressed firm and vice versa. Hence, the theories behind Zmijewski model are contradictory. Therefore, the hypothesis H_{11}: The models Altman's Z-score and Zmijewski's Score contradict each other is true.

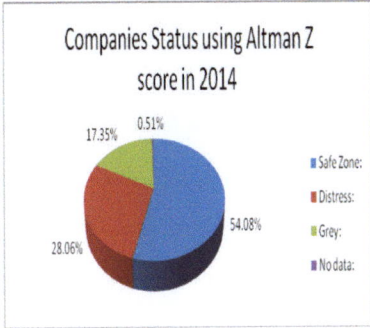

Figure 11. Companies Status of the Altman Z-score in 2014

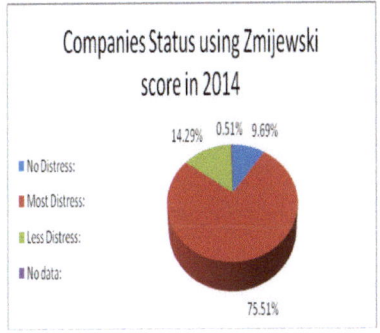

Figure 12. Companies Status of the Zmijewski score in 2014

The hypotheses, H_{02}: Bankruptcy does not occur in two years if Zmijewski's Score is positive, and H_{12}: Bankruptcy can occur in two years if Zmijewski's Score is negative are null in case of Kuwait as there are no established bankruptcy laws and all firms are in operation despite the presence of distress factor. However, if Chapter 11 existed, approximately 75.51% of the firms in 2014 would be headed towards bankruptcy, according to the Zmijewski model.

Summary of Results

To summarize, the results from the Altman Z-score model, the firms in the secure zone kept increasing from 15.31% in 2009, 19.90% in 2010, 47.45% in 2011, 48.47% in 2012, 51.53% in 2013, and 54.08% in 2014. This signifies that the listed firms in Kuwait Stock Exchange are growing to be financially secure as the year's progress since the financial crisis of 2008. The firms in between the secure and distressed zone increased from 9.18% in 2009, 12.76% in 2010, and 16.33% in 2011, 18.88% in 2012, 20.92% in 2013, and further declined to 17.35% in 2014. The distressed firms kept increasing at a rapid pace of 16.33% in 2009, 16.84% in 2010, 35.20% in 2011, and 32.14% in 2012, declined to 27.04% in 2013, and increased to 28.06% in 2014. This points out that the majority of the firms listed on the Kuwait Stock Exchange are not performing well financially.

On the contrary, the Zmijewski score results showed that the distress level of the listed firms in Kuwait Stock Exchange kept increasing from 24.49% in 2009 to 75.51% in 2014. This signifies that 75.51% should be hitting bankruptcy. The financially secure firms ranged from 8.67% in 2009 to 9.69% in 2014. However, 79.90% ratio in the Zmijewski model was positive, showing non-distressed firms. Hence, a contradiction has occurred in the results of this model.

Chapter 5: Conclusions and Recommendations

Summary of the Results

The researcher concludes the final chapter of this paper by presenting the summary of the results, discussion of the results, conclusions and practical recommendations, and lastly, recommendations for further research.

The Kuwait financial market has been untapped and unexplored by potential investors. In order to explore, financial performance of the listed firms on the Kuwait Stock Exchange must be assessed. The Kuwait Stock Exchange consist of of 206 firms. This assessment was conducted using Altman Z-score and Zmijewski score models to predict the performance and the bankruptcy rate on 196 listed firms. The researcher used quantitative methodology using published financial data from the annual reports of the listed firms and financial statements from the Kuwait Stock Exchange website. The data were analyzed for the period 2009-2014 after the financial crisis of 2008. A certain criteria scale was used by both models to calculate the results.

The results of Altman Z-score shows that approx. 39.46% firms average for the period 2009-2014 were financially secure, approx. 25.94% firms average for the period 2009-2014 were distressed, approx. 15.90% firms average for the period 2009-2014 were neither secure nor distressed, and the balance 18.71% firms approx. on an average had no available data. While the results of Zmijewski score shows approx. 11.22% firms average for the period 2009-2014 were financially secure, approx. 57.74% firms average for the period 2009-2014 are bankrupt, approx. 12.33% firms average for the period 2009-2014 were neither secure nor safe, and the balance 18.71% firms approx. on an average had no available data.

Discussion of the Results

Four hypotheses were created for this research. The measures used for predicting these hypotheses were via Altman Z-score criterion model and Zmijeski score model. The criterion scale used for Altman Z-score model was Safe Zone = Z > 2.99 (risk free); Distress Zone = Z < 1.81 (bankruptcy); and Grey Zone = 1.81 < = Z < = 2.99 (at risk). For banks, the Altman Z-score model criteria was Z > 5.85 Safe Zone; 4.35 < Z < 5.85 Grey Zone; and Z < 4.35 Distress Zone. Alternatively, for Zmijewski score model, firms with positive scores were shown as non-distressed, while negative scores showed distressed firms. In the following section of this chapter, the main findings for each hypothesis are reviewed by the researcher followed by discussion and analysis of these findings.

H_{01}: **The models Altman's Z-score and Zmijewski's Score do not contradict each other**

This hypothesis is null and inconclusive as Altman's Z-score and Zmijewski's score were in contradiction for all the years from 2009-2014.

H_{11}: **The models Altman's Z-score and Zmijewski's Score contradict each other.**

For the years 2009 and 2010, the models Altman's Z-score and Zmijewski's Score predicted different data. In 2009 and 2010, the risk free sectors were banks, consumer services, consumer goods, industrials, basic materials, and oil and gas. The distressed sectors were financial services, telecom, and health care. Around 59.18% of the firms have no information for the year 2009, and 50.51% in 2010. In 2009, the Altman's Z-score model indicated 15.31% firms were safe while, Zmijewski's score model showed 8.67%. The Altman's Z-score model indicated 16.33% firms were distressed while, Zmijewski's score model showed 24.49%. Finally, the Altman's Z-score model indicated 9.18% firms were neither safe nor distressed while, Zmijewski's score model showed 7.65%. In 2010, the Altman's Z-score model indicated 19.90% firms were safe while, Zmijewski's score model showed 11.73%. The Altman's Z-score model indicated 16.84% firms were distressed while, Zmijewski's score model showed 30.61%. Finally, the Altman's Z-score model indicated 12.76% firms were neither safe nor distressed while, Zmijewski's score model showed 7.14%.

For the years 2011-2014, the models Altman's Z-score and Zmijewski's Score predicted different data. In 2011, the risk free sectors were oil and gas, basic materials, industrials, consumer goods, consumer services, banks, technology, and parallel market. The distressed sectors were real estate, financial services, telecom, and health care. The Altman's Z-score model indicated 47.45% firms were safe while, Zmijewski's score model showed 15.31%. The Altman's Z-score model indicated 35.20% firms were distressed while, Zmijewski's score model showed 68.88%. Finally, the Altman's Z-score model indicated 16.33% firms were neither safe nor distressed while, Zmijewski's score model showed 14.80%.

In 2012, the risk free sectors were oil and gas, basic materials, industrials, consumer goods, consumer services, banks, technology, and parallel market. The distressed sectors were real estate, financial services, telecom, and health care. The number of firms that were financially secure are 48.47% in Altman's Z-score model when compared to 12.24% in Zmijewski's score model. The Altman's Z-score model indicated 32.14% firms were distressed while, Zmijewski's score model showed 70.41%. Finally, the Altman's Z-score model indicated 18.88% firms were neither safe nor distressed while, Zmijewski's score model showed 16.84%.

In 2013, the risk free sectors were oil and gas, basic materials, industrials, consumer goods, consumer services, technology, and parallel market. The distressed sectors were real estate, financial services, telecom, and health care. The number of firms that were financially secure are 51.53% in Altman's Z-score model when compared to 9.69% in Zmijewski's score model. The Altman's Z-score model indicated 27.04% firms were distressed while, Zmijewski's score model showed 76.53%. Finally, the Altman's Z-score model indicated 20.92% firms were neither safe nor distressed while, Zmijewski's score model showed 13.27%.

In 2014, the risk free sectors were basic materials, industrials, consumer goods, technology, and parallel market. The distressed sectors were oil and gas, real estate, financial services, telecom, consumer services, and health care. The number of firms that were financially secure are 54.08% in Altman's Z-score model when compared to 9.69% in Zmijewski's score model in 2014. The Altman's Z-score model indicated 28.06% firms were distressed while, Zmijewski's score model showed 75.51%. Finally, the Altman's Z-score model indicated 17.35% firms were neither safe nor distressed while, Zmijewski's score model showed 14.29%. Hence, the hypothesis was true in all the years from 2011-2014.

H_{02}: **Bankruptcy does not occur in two years if Zmijewski's Score is positive.**

Due to the contradiction in theories of Zmijewski score results and absence of bankruptcy laws in Kuwait, this hypothesis is null and inconclusive.

H_{12}: **Bankruptcy can occur in two years if Zmijewski's Score is negative.**

Due to the contradiction in theories of Zmijewski score results and absence of bankruptcy laws in Kuwait, this hypothesis is null and inconclusive. However, with the established and implemented bankruptcy laws in Kuwait, this can be predicted using Zmijewski score model.

Conclusions and Practical Recommendations

A primary conclusion of this exploration is that it is possible to predict accurately the level of financial distress in Kuwait using the financial data from annual reports and financial statements from the Kuwait Stock Exchange website. However, the bankruptcy model

Zmijewski score, produced contradictory results. Hence, the bankruptcy rate hypotheses were inconclusive as no bankruptcy laws exist in Kuwait.

The dependable model in the case of Kuwait is Altman's Z score Model showed 54.08% financially secure firms in 2014 and roughly 28.06% firms distressed in 2014. The balance of the firms were neither distressed nor secure financially. The Zmijewski score Model was the worst model to apply in Kuwait.

This study provides insight into the financial distress level in Kuwait. The high level of distress shows that major changes are necessary in firms. This also shows that the operations are not running smooth. The sectors that are performing well for investment: petroleum, food, slaughter houses, and banks. Surprisingly, the distressed firms continue to operate despite the losses. Real estate and telecommunication sectors are the worst performers, and yet, they continue to expand their projects/operations respectively.

Bankruptcy laws, like Chapter 11, is required for firms operating in distress. This allows the business entrepreneurs to default and fresh start their new operations. New competition in the market will help the existing firms to rise up to the new business trends and to improve their functionality. This will improve the market and attract more profitable investments around the globe.

Recommendations for Further Research

According to Kim (2002), the blow of catastrophic events can be examined by computing change on the whole default probability of firms after the event. The continuous type of credit risk measure has the higher foretelling power to recognize financially distressed firms, one year prior to the bankruptcy because of growing investor involvement and enhanced market transparency in the recent market. This credit risk measure helps to estimate the financial impact on different industries, for instance, the China market crash, has an impact on oil and gold industry.

The option-based measure is another alternative prediction tool for scholars and practitioners. However, the researcher did not provide evidence that the option-based model is a better predictor than variables in Altman's Z-score model. This measure is applicable only to a certain industry, such as manufacturing and retail trade, and the possibility of modification of the measure remains promising but challenging (Kim, 2002).

The outcomes of the evaluation using the Altman model for the period 2011-2014, revealed that on an average 25.94% firms are financially distressed, while the Zmijewski model identified 57.74% firms as bankrupt. Thus, the models Altman and Zmijewski were in contradiction for the period 2009-2014. As for the period 2009-2010, no data were available for approx. 54.85% firms. Hence, it is recommended that firms assess their financial performance using both models of Altman and Zmijewski. The Altman Z-score model will assess whether the firm is safe and sound, while Zmijewski will predict if the firm is headed towards bankruptcy. The Zmijewski score model can be successful only if the bankruptcy laws well established and implemented. This will prevent in the contradiction of theories in case of Zmijeski model. Therefore, the results with respect to Zmijewski model are inconclusive at this point. Future researchers can analyze the bankruptcy rate in Kuwait using the bankruptcy laws, whenever established. They can create their own criterion for bankruptcy level. Therefore, in further studies, new combinations of financial ratios could be added to the Altman Z-score model in order to search for better model designs and reach more satisfactory results based on different sectors/industries based in Kuwait. This paper could challenge and encourage a new platform to the prospective researchers for developing and enhancing models that are applicable to the

countries in the Gulf region.

References

Aasen, M. R. (2011). *Applying Altman's Z-Score to the financial crisis. An empirical study of financial distress on Oslo stock exchange.* Retrieved from http://brage.bibsys.no/xmlui/bitstream/handle/11250/169347/Aasen%202011.pdf?sequence=1

Al-Yaqout, A. (2013, November 3). Door to total foreign ownership in companies opened in Kuwait. *Kuwait Times.* Retrieved from http://news.kuwaittimes.net/door-total-foreign -ownership-companies-opened-kuwait/

Alareeni, B., & Branson, J. (2012). Predicting listed companies' failure in Jordan using Altman Models: A case study. *International Journal of Business and Management, 8*(1), 113-126. Retrieved from http://www.ccsenet.org/journal/index.php/ijbm/article/view/20560

Altman, E. (1968). Financial ratios, discriminant analysis and the prediction of corporate bankruptcy. *The Journal of Finance, 23*(4), 589. Retrieved from http://onlinelibrary.wiley.com/doi/10.1111/j.1540-6261.1968.tb00843.x/pdf

Altman, E., & Hotchkiss, E. (2006). *Corporate financial distress and bankruptcy.* Retrieved from http://down.cenet.org.cn/upfile/21/200954235115167.pdf

Avenhuis, J. (2013). *Testing the generalizability of the bankruptcy prediction models of Altman, Ohlson and Zmijewski for Dutch listed and large non-listed firms.* Retrieved from http://essay.utwente.nl/64326/1/MSc_Oude%20Avenhuis.pdf

Aymz, L. (2010). *Earning the extra buck: how to invest in Kuwait stock exchange II.* Retrieved from http://mybloogle.com/earning-the-extra-buck-how-to-invest-in-kuwait-stock-exchange-ii/

Balasundaram, N. (2009). An investigation of financial soundness of listed manufacturing

    companies in Sri Lanka: An application of Altman's model. *Economic Sciences Series,*

    61(4), 19-25. Retrieved

    fromhttp://web.b.ebscohost.com/ehost/pdfviewer/pdfviewer?sid=4209cf9d-3c81-4f06-

    a1f1-ca3cc6ae14b5%40sessionmgr115&vid=11&hid=101

Beaver, W. (1966). Financial ratios as predictors of failure. *Journal of Accounting Research*, 4,

    71. Retrieved from http://www.jstor.org/stable/2490171?seq=1#page_scan_tab_contents

Bell, T. (1997). Neural nets or the logit model? A comparison of each model's ability to predict

    commercial bank failures. *International Journal of Intelligent Systems in Accounting,*

    Finance & Management, 6(3), 249-264. doi:

    10.1002/(SICI)10991174(199709)6:3<249::AID-ISAF125>3.0.CO;2-H

Bemmann, M. (2005). Improving the comparability of insolvency predictions. *Dresden*

    Discussion Paper Series in Economics, 1-148. Retrieved from

    http://econwpa.repec.org/eps/fin/papers/0506/0506017.pdf

Berk, J., & DeMarzo, P. (2011). *Corporate Finance (2nd ed.).* Berkeley, California. Prentice

    Hall

Calandro, J. (2007). Considering the utility of Altman's Z-Score as a strategic assessment and

    performance management tool. *Strategy & Leadership, 35*(5), 37-43.

    doi:10.1108/10878570710819206

Charles, O., & Goodluck, A. (2009). *Financial ratios and the state of health of Nigerian banks.*

    Retrieved from

    http://www.unilag.edu.ng/opendoc.php?sno=19466&doctype=doc&docname=FINANCI

AL%20RATIOS%20AND%20THE%20STATE%20OF%20HEALTH%20OF%20NIGE
RIAN%20BANKS

Chouhan, V., Chandra, B., & Goswami, S. (2014). Predicting financial stability of select BSE

companies revisiting Altman Z-score. *International Letters of Social and Humanistic*

Sciences, 26, 92-105. Retrieved from http://www.scipress.com/ILSHS.26.92.pdf

Chung, K. C., Tan, S. S., & Holdsworth, D. K. (2008). Insolvency prediction model using

multivariate discriminant analysis and artificial neural network for the finance industry in

New Zealand. *International Journal of Business and Management, 3*(1), 19-28. Retrieved

from

http://poseidon01.ssrn.com/delivery.php?ID=3730870700221000130890961271270040l

801708802507206300307402211709202410700211209700204501603004204102702600

302009410212609511805508105550540070830931081241270751110580580160980908

61090750700710820090710880911261090051260060910821080860910680720l3085&

EXT=pdf

Deakin, E. (1972). A discriminant analysis of predictors of business failure. *Journal of*

Accounting Research, 10(1), 167-179. doi:10.2307/2490225

Definition of 'Speculation' (n.d.). *The Economic Times*. Retrieved from

http://economictimes.indiatimes.com/definition/speculation

Delice, A. (2010). The sampling issues in quantitative research. *Educational Sciences: Theory*

and Practice, 10(4), 2001-2018. Retrieved from

http://files.eric.ed.gov/fulltext/EJ919871.pdf

Diakomihalis, M. (2012). The accuracy of Altman's models in predicting hotel bankruptcy. *International Journal of Accounting and Financial Reporting, 2*(2), 96-113. Retrieved from http://www.macrothink.org/journal/index.php/ijafr/article/viewFile/2367/2204

Dissertation India. (n.d.). *Determining sample size in quantitative research.* Retrieved from http://www.dissertationindia.com/determining-sample-size.html

Fitzpatrick, P. (1932). *A comparison of ratios of successful industrial enterprises with those of failed firms*, 10-12, 598-605, 656-662, 727-731. Retrieved from http://www.worldcat.org/title/comparison-of-the-ratios-of-successful-industrial-enterprises-with-those-of-failed-companies/oclc/6284198

Gerantonis, N.,Vergos, K., & Christopoulos, A. (2009). Can Altman Z-score models predict business failures in Greece?. *Research Journal of International Studies*, 12, 21-28. Retrieved from http://www.academia.edu/338693/Can_Altman_Z Score_Models_Predict_Business_Failures_In_Greece

Gharaibeh, M., Sartawi, I., & Daradkah, D. (2013). The Applicability of corporate failure models to emerging economies: Evidence from Jordan. *Interdisciplinary Journal of Contemporary Research in Business, 5*(4), 313-325. Retrieved from http://journalarchieves35.webs.com/313-325.pdf

Grice, J., & Dugan, M. (2003). *Re-estimations of the Zmijewski and Ohlson bankruptcy prediction models*. Retrieved from http://www.sciencedirect.com/science/article/pii/S0882611003200043

Gurau, T. (2013). *A model of bankruptcy prediction: calibration of Atman's Z-score for Japan, 1-29.* Retrieved from http://thesis.eur.nl/pub/13759/Gurau-T.-340938.pdf

Hassan, K., Al-Sultan, W., & Al-Saleem, J. (2003). *Stock market efficiency in the Gulf Cooperation Council Countries (GCC): The case of Kuwait stock exchange*. Retrieved from

http://www.researchgate.net/publication/242286464_Stock_Market_Efficiency_in_the_G

ulf_Cooperation_Council_Countries_(GCC)_The_Case_of_Kuwait_Stock_Exchange

Ibrahim, F. (2013). *World bank supports strengthening of Kuwait's insolvency and creditor/debtor regime*. Retrieved from http://www.worldbank.org/en/news/press-

release/2013/06/03/world-bank-supports-strengthening-of-kuwait-insolvency-and-

creditor-debtor-regime

Ijaz, M., Hameed, Z., Hunjra, A., Maqbool, A., & Azam, R. (2013). Assessing the financial

failure using z-score and current ratio: A case of sugar sector listed companies of Karachi

stock exchange. *World Applies Sciences Journal, 23*(6), 863-870.

doi:10.5829/idosi.wasj.2013.23.06.2243

Kida, T. (1980). An investigation into auditors' continuity and related qualification judgments.

Journal of Accounting Research, 18(2), 506-523. doi: 10.2307/2490590

Kim, B. (2002). *Altman's Z-score and Option-based approach for credit risk measure

(Bankruptcy prediction: Book value or Market Value?)*, 1-35. Retrieved from

http://www.iksa.or.kr/search/down.php?r_code=1100002&num=921

Kpodoh, B. (2009). *Bankruptcy and financial distress prediction in the mobile telecom industry*.

Retrieved from http://bth.divaportal.org/smash/get/diva2:832030/FULLTEXT01.pdf

Kumar, R., & Kumar, K. (2012). A comparison of bankruptcy models. *International Journal of

Marketing, Financial Services & Management Research, 1*(4), 76-86. Retrieved from

http://indianresearchjournals.com/pdf/IJMFSMR/2012/April/10.pdf

Kuwait Stock Exchange. (n.d.). *About KSE - Who we are?* Retrieved from

http://www.kse.com.kw/EN/AboutKSE/Pages/WhoWeAre.aspx

Kuwait Stock Exchange. (n.d.). *Foreign investor.* Retrieved from

http://www.kse.com.kw/EN/AboutKSE/Pages/ForeignInvestor.aspx

Lexology. (2015). *Kuwait considers new insolvency legislation.* Retrieved from

http://www.lexology.com/library/detail.aspx?g=435f637c-b2d6-47fc-b02a-4a4f0a55f11d

Li, J. (2012). Prediction of corporate bankruptcy from 2008 through 2011. *Journal of Accounting

and Finance, 12*(1), 31-41. Retrieved from http://t.www.na-

businesspress.com/JAF/LiJ_Web12_1_.pdf

McCallum, J. (2010). *Using Z score to manage financial health.* Retrieved from

http://bankinnovation.net/2010/07/using-z-score-to-manage-financial-health/

Meeampol, S., Lerskullawat, P., Wongsorntham, A., Srinammuang, P., Rodpetch, V., & Noonoi,

R. (2014). *Applying emerging market Z-score model to predict bankruptcy: A case study

of listed companies in the stock exchange of Thailand (Set)*, 1227-1237. Retrieved from

http://www.toknowpress.net/ISBN/978-961-6914-09-3/.../ML14-724.pdf

Miller, W. (2009). *Comparing Models of Corporate Bankruptcy Prediction: Distance to Default

vs. Z-Score,* 1-20. Retrieved from

https://corporate.morningstar.com/us/documents/MethodologyDocuments/MethodologyP

apers/CompareModelsCorporateBankruptcyPrediction.pdf

Moghadam, A. G., Zadeh, F. N., & Fard, M. M. G. (2010). *Review of the prediction power of

Altman and Ohlson models in predicting bankruptcy of listed companies in Tehran stock

exchange.* Retrieved from http://www.mbaforum.ir/download/mba/m/7th/236.pdf

Mohammed, A., & Kim-Soon, N. (2012). Using Altman's model and current ratio to assess the

financial status of companies quoted in the Malaysian stock exchange. *International*

Journal of Scientific and Research Publications, 2(7), 1-11. Retrieved from

http://eprints.uthm.edu.my/2911/1/Ali_Abusalah_Elmabrok_Mohammed_1.pdf

Muthukumar, G., & M., Sekar. (2014). Fiscal fitness of select automobile companies in India:

Application of Z-score and Springate models. *Vilakshan: The XIMB Journal of*

Management, 11(2), 19-34. Retrieved from

http://web.b.ebscohost.com/ehost/pdfviewer/pdfviewer?sid=1037067f-daad-48b9-bc21-

7d04e17f7e2f%40sessionmgr114&vid=2&hid=118

Odipo, M. K. , & Sitati, A. (2008). *Evaluation of applicability of Altman's revised model in*

prediction of financial distress: A case of companies quoted in the Nairobi stock

exchange. Retrieved from

http://erepository.uonbi.ac.ke/bitstream/handle/11295/9904/aibuma2011-

submission236%20%20EVALUATION%20OF%20APPLICABILITY%20OF%20ALT

MAN%27S%20REVISED%20MODEL%20IN%20PREDICTION%20OF%20FINANCI

AL%20DISTRESS.pdf?sequence=1

Odom, M., & Sharda, R. (1990). A neural network model for bankruptcy prediction.

International Joint Conference on Neural Networks and San Diego, CA, USA, 163-168.

Retrieved from

http://ieeexplore.ieee.org/xpl/articleDetails.jsp?tp=&arnumber=5726669&url=http%3A%

2F%2Fieeexplore.ieee.org%2Fxpls%2Fabs_all.jsp%3Farnumber%3D5726669

Ohlson, J. (1980). Financial Ratios and the probabilistic prediction of bankruptcy. *Journal of Accounting Research, 18*(1), 109. Retrieved from http://teaching.ust.hk/~ismt551j/project2/Ohlson.pdf

Omet, G., & Mashharawe, F. (n.d.). *The capital structure choice in tax contrasting environments: evidence from the Jordanian, Kuwaiti, Omani and Saudi corporate sectors.* Retrieved http://www.erf.org.eg/CMS/uploads/pdf/1184761710_Omet.pdf

Onofrei, M., & Lupu, D. (2012). Controversies regarding the utilization of Altman model in Romania. *Journal of Public Administration, Finance and Law*, 1, 33-42. Retrieved from http://www.jopafl.com/uploads/CONTROVERSIES-REGARDING-THE-UTILIZATION-OF-ALTMAN-MODEL-IN-ROMANIA.pdf

Onyeiwu, C. (2009). *Financial statement as instrument for predicting corporate health in Nigeria.* Retrieved from http://www.unilag.edu.ng/opendoc.php?sno=19468&doctype=doc&docname=FINANCIAL%20STATEMENT%20AS%20INSTRUMENT%20FOR%20PREDICTING

Oxford Business Group. (2015). *Kuwait: Building for the future.* Retrieved from http://www.oxfordbusinessgroup.com/kuwait-2015

Park, J. (2012). *Developing and validating an instrument to measure college students' inferential reasoning in statistics: An argument-based approach to validation*, 1-304. Retrieved from http://iase-web.org/documents/dissertations/12.Park.Dissertation.pdf

Pitrova, K. (2011). Possibilities of the Altman zeta model application to Czech firms. *Economics and Management*, 3, 66-76. Retrieved from http://www.ekonomie-management.cz/download/1346065779_8f30/2011_03_pitrova.pdf

Pongsatat, S., Ramage, J., & Lawrence, H. (2004). Bankruptcy prediction for large and small

firms in Asia: A comparison of Ohlson and Altman. *Journal of Accounting and*

Corporate Governance, 1(2), 1-13. Retrieved from http://jacg.rd.fcu.edu.tw/dl/1201.pdf

Portland State University. (n.d.). *Quantitative research: Reliability*

285-298. doi:10.1057/jdhf.2008.22

Scott, D. L. (2003). *Bankruptcy*. Retrieved from

http://financialdictionary.thefreedictionary.com/Bankruptcy

Sharif, A., & Benmeleh, Y. (2015, March 8). Kuwait stocks lead Gulf market drop as oil sinks

most in 8 weeks. *Bloomberg*. Retrieved from

http://www.bloomberg.com/news/articles/2015-03-08/dubai-stocks-lead-gulf-market-

drop-as-oil-sinks-most-in-8-weeks

Shumway, T. (2001). Forecasting bankruptcy more accurately: A simple hazard model. *The*

Journal of Business, 74(1), 101- 124. Retrieved from

http://homes.chass.utoronto.ca/~szhou/print/ForcastingBankruptcyHazardModel.pdf

Sikimic, S. (2015). *Profile: What is the GCC?* Retrieved from

http://www.middleeasteye.net/news/profile-what-gcc-18030284

SlideShare. (2011). Berk Chapter 16: Financial Distress. Retrieved from

http://www.slideshare.net/HerbMeiberger/berkchapter16financialdistress?from_action=sa

ve

Sulub, S.A. (2014). Testing the predictive power of Altman's revised Z' model: The

case of 10 multinational companies. *Research Journal of Finance and Accounting, 5*(21),

174-184. Retrieved from

http://www.iiste.org/Journals/index.php/RJFA/article/download/17586/17872

Taffler, R. (1983). The assessment of company solvency and performance using a statistical

    model. *Accounting and Business Research, 15*(3), 295-308.

    doi:10.1080/00014788.1983.9729767

The Free Dictionary. (2009). *Altman Z-score.* Retrieved from http://financial-

    dictionary.thefreedictionary.com/Altman+Z-

The Free Dictionary. (2011). *Asset.* Retrieved from http://www.thefreedictionary.com/asset

The Free Dictionary. (2011). *Distress.* Retrieved from http://www.thefreedictionary.com/distress

The Free Dictionary. (2011). *Hot money.* Retrieved from

    http://www.thefreedictionary.com/hot+money

The Securities House K.S.C.C. (n.d.). *About Kuwait stock exchange.* Retrieved from

    http://www.sh.com.kw/kst1.htm

Twycross, A., & Shields, L. (2004). Validity and reliability - What's it all about? Part 1 Validity

    in quantitative studies. *Pediatric Nursing, 16*(9), 28. Retrieved from

    http://www.ncbi.nlm.nih.gov/pubmed/15633276

Wang, Y., & Campbell, M. (2010). Business failure prediction for publicly listed companies in

    China. *Journal of Business & Management, 16*(1), 75-880. Retrieved from

    http://web.a.ebscohost.com/abstract?direct=true&profile=ehost&scope=site&authtype=cr

    awler&jrnl=1535668X&AN=51003323&h=G1L6ema5jyygqFGRtygwArngSdsjFWP49n

    8R87vxc6hUDUbBIcT5ZuZDyGba9u9%2fhl2M9Un8Cq4xl0boK2YKHQ%3d%3d&crl

    =f&resultNs=AdminWebAuth&resultLocal=ErrCrlNotAuth&crlhashurl=login.aspx%3fd

    irect%3dtrue%26profile%3dehost%26scope%3dsite%26authtype%3dcrawler%26jrnl%3

    d1535668X%26AN%3d51003323

Waqas, H., Hussain, N., & Anees, U. (2014). Zmijewski financial distress prediction model and

    its predictability, A case of Karachi stock exchange. *Journal of Basic and Applied*

    Scientific Research, 4(4), 155-163. Retrieved from

    http://textroad.com/pdf/JBASR/J.%20Basic.%20Appl.%20Sci.%20Res.,%204(4)155-

    163,%202014.pdf

World Bank. (n.d.). *Data by country Kuwait.* Retrieved from

    http://data.worldbank.org/country/kuwait

YCharts. (n.d.). *Zmijewski score.* Retrieved from

    http://ycharts.com/glossary/terms/zmijewski_score

Zmijewski, M. (1984). Methodological issues related to the estimation of financial distress

    prediction models. *Journal of Accounting Research, 22*(Supplement), 59-86.

    doi:10.2307/2490859